RENEWED ON THE RUN

Renewed
on the Run

MARION DUCKWORTH

VICTOR BOOKS®

A DIVISION OF SCRIPTURE PRESS PUBLICATIONS INC.
USA CANADA ENGLAND

Recommended Dewey Decimal Classification: 227.92
Suggested Subject Heading: BIBLE, N.T., 1 PETER

Library of Congress Catalog Card Number: 91-65453
ISBN: 0-89693-878-6

1 2 3 4 5 6 7 8 9 10 Printing/Year 95 94 93 92 91

VICTOR BOOKS
A division of SP Publications, Inc.
Wheaton, Illinois 60187

CONTENTS

INTRODUCTION

"I'm busy—that's for sure. But some days I'm not so sure I'm accomplishing very much!"

Your sympathetic friend groans knowingly. "You're not the only one. Busyness must be the new female disease."

Just maybe. The symptoms? A vague discontent as we fall into bed at night, for one. *Life is a rat race and the rats are winning!*

Women in American society today are more active in life around them than in any other era. Over 50 percent of them work at jobs outside the home, and by the year 2000, the figure may reach 75 percent. The majority of American women also do most of the housework and care for family members, from preschoolers to aged parents.

Life crowds us to the wall. Today's *urgent* list includes picking up supplies for the businesses we're starting, and parts that our husbands need to repair the plumbing. Then there's the dog to take to the vet, Mom to take shopping, the car to take to be tuned up, the lawn to fertilize, and the garage to clean. Says Barb, a single parent who races from job to home to job again, "I've lost my sense of purpose."

First Peter was written just for women like that. The lives of the first-century Christians in Asia Minor to whom it was addressed were chaotic. They had been uprooted from their familiar Palestinian surroundings where they lived predictable lives, grinding grain with aunts and cousins and visiting at the well with villagers they'd known for years. Suddenly these believers were living in a society that did not honor Judeo-Christian values. Daily they were intermingling with people who didn't want to hear about Jesus Christ, the Savior of the world, thank you very much.

The outlook for them was not good. They were suffering from persecution and its consequences and, under Nero, life would get

7

worse, not better. It wasn't just uprootedness that troubled them; it was a no-nonsense intolerance toward them that made them shiver.

The same thing is happening in our world. The harassment Christians experience may be more subtle because it comes from a society that touts itself as progressive, informed, and unbiased. But Paul foresaw today clearly. "Mark this: There will be terrible times in the last days" (2 Tim. 3:1). Our lives today are all-of-a-piece with our first-century sisters because, like them, we are oddities in the world.

Whether you are feeling subtle (or not-so-subtle) persecution for your faith, or whether you need your purpose for living restored, you will benefit from this study. *Your Father Writes* is an inductive study. *Reflections Along the Way* contains insights to help you look more deeply into each subject. *Day by Day with God*, written appointment-book style, assigns journaling for each weekday. *Between Father and Daughter* offers prayer suggestions to take you through the week.

If you are studying on your own, make a point of sharing what you are learning with someone else. You will solidify lessons in your mind while blessing your friend.

If you are part of a group, you will find it most helpful to work through the study questions on your own before the group meets. Then you will be ready to share what you learned from the passage and how it applies to your life, plus any questions that arose as you studied. Members will profit from hearing one another's insights and perceptions.

Using the study questions, work through the Scripture passage *before* you read the narrative section; in this way, your initial findings will all be original.

Throughout the study, remember that the Holy Spirit is your teacher. Ask Him to give you eyes to see His truth and a spirit ready to obey it.

As you come across questions that call for you to connect the truth of the passage to your own life, answer them prayerfully. Let the Spirit guide you in applying God's Word to your life. When you find something in the passage that makes you feel grateful to God, thank Him! When something leads you to praise Him, stop and do so! When the Spirit points to something in your life that doesn't measure up to what you're reading in Scripture, let Him speak to you. Confess any sin and allow God to cleanse you and lead you in the right direction.

To be properly equipped for each study, you will need three Bible translations (including your favorite), this study guide, and a dictionary, plus any other materials named by the leader (if you have one). You will also need a notebook in which to record your thoughts and discoveries from *Day by Day with God* and *Between Father and Daughter*. You could also use it to list prayer requests in a group setting plus their resolutions.

PREPARED TO BE AMBASSADORS
1 Peter 1:1-12

YOUR FATHER WRITES

Day 1: A letter from home Read 1 Peter 1:1-12. Review verse 1a.
1. What friend or family member wrote you the most helpful letter when you were once away from home? Why was it helpful? What did it reveal about the writer's attitude toward you?

2. Peter's purpose in writing this letter was to encourage Christians to be faithful in difficult circumstances—particularly persecution. Jot down encouraging words or phrases from 1 Peter.
   Inheritance which is imperishable

3. Peter calls himself "an apostle" in 1:1. What's the dictionary definition of that word? Who does 2 Timothy 3:16 say is the real author of 1 Peter? What four things can you expect Scripture to do for you? What will be the result for the woman of God?

Day 2: Identified Read 1 Peter 1:1-2.
1. Imagine that you had to leave your home indefinitely and could take only a medium-sized suitcase. List the six most important items you would pack. Why would you choose them?

2. The people to whom this letter was originally addressed had to leave their homes. On a map of Bible lands (check the back of your Bible for one), locate the countries in Asia Minor to which these believers moved.

11

3. The recipients of the letter are described as "scattered." Is your extended family scattered? Name the cities in which they live. List five places where you regularly spend time. Write a note to a first-century woman and tell her how you relate to her.

4. "Scattered" also describes seeds which are sown. Think of yourself as someone chosen to sow the seeds of the Gospel. What do you learn from Psalm 126:5-6? Luke 8:4-15? 1 Corinthians 3:6-9?

5. In 1:1, Peter describes the believers as God's "elect strangers." What synonym for "elect" is used in verse 2? What four facts do we learn about our election in verse 2? Likewise, a political candidate is elected to do certain things. What are some of them? What new thoughts do you have about being elected?

6. In Greek the word for "stranger" (1:1) means "resident foreigner" — like an ambassador from another country. Since *ambassador* came from words that meant "mission" and "servant," how does this shape the way you see yourself? Reflect on the fact that you are scattered, elected, and a stranger. What general conclusions do you draw about your purpose for living?

Day 3: Outfitted Read 1 Peter 1:3-5.
1. Suppose you were going on a day's trip and had to be ready to participate in a wide variety of activities. Describe your outfit.

First Peter 1:3-5 describes four ways God has outfitted us to live successfully as resident aliens in this world. Describe how each way enables us to live for God. Look up the additional Scripture references for further help.
   ❦ *New birth.* Synonym: regeneration. Ezekiel 36:26-27; John 1:12-13.

❦ *Living hope.* Synonyms: vital, energizing, confident, or expectant hope. Colossians 1:27; Titus 2:11-13.

❦ *Inheritance in heaven.* Synonyms: legacy or possession. What was Israel's inheritance? (see Josh. 11:23) What things can you think of that are included in your inheritance?

❦ *Shielded by God's power.* Synonyms: guarded, watched over. Says Kenneth S. Wuest, "The guard is never changed. It is on duty twenty-four hours a day, year in and year out until we arrive safe in heaven" (*Wuest's Word Studies*, Vol. II, Grand Rapids: Eerdmans, 1942, p. 22). What do you learn about God's protection of you in Genesis 28:15? Second Timothy 1:12? Jude 24-25?

2. How will you be better able to function in the following situations because you are so equipped?
   ❦ Your husband quits his job because of an ethical problem.

   ❦ You're the only Christian on a service organization board.

   ❦ You're falsely accused of wrongdoing by an employer or acquaintance.

Day 4: Trials Read 1 Peter 1:6-9.
1. Describe one of the worst problems you've ever had on a trip.

We Christians experience all kinds of trials in this world. One reason is that we have a different value system than non-Christians. Look up *trial* in the dictionary and write a definition that applies in verse 6. What word describes how we may feel in a trial?

2. For first-century Christians, these trials resulted in social and, then, physical persecution. From the passages below, name the people who went through trials, the reasons for the trials, and the kinds of trials they suffered.

	Person(s)	Reason	Kind of trial
Exodus 1:1-14			
Daniel 6:7-28			
Philippians 1:12-14			

3. Why does God let us go through these experiences? (1 Peter 1:7)

Reflect on the example below and note what you learn about the testing through which God allows us to go:

A lab puts an automobile through rigorous testing to see if it lives up to the manufacturer's advertised claims. Consider the lab's purpose and the fact that the manufacturer will correct any flaws in the car's construction.

What's the reward for remaining faithful? (v. 7)

4. Our faith is rooted in Christ, whom Peter saw but whom we have not. Name two living persons whom you haven't met but whom you respect and admire. Explain your choices. Tell why you love Jesus though you haven't physically seen Him. Rewrite verse 8 in your own words and express your own attitude toward the Lord.

Romans 5.1 —

Day 5: Privileged Read 1 Peter 1:10-12.
1. Old Testament prophets, such as Isaiah, foretold things about the

14

coming Messiah and His converts that they (the prophets) couldn't understand (vv. 10-11). Imagine that you are Isaiah writing Isaiah 7:14 and 53:3-6. What specific statements might be mystifying to you? What reflections would you, as Isaiah, write about the prohecies in your journal?

2. After God provided the kind of insight found in verse 12, what might you write in your journal—this time, as yourself?

3. List words from verse 12 that point out how privileged you are. Next to these privileges, write how they influence the way you live as a resident alien and ambassador.

REFLECTIONS ALONG THE WAY

The housedress store was one of my girlhood treasures. Since it was on a corner in Coney Island where we lived, Mama and I passed it often. The window displays were a rich aunt among poor relatives. No cut-rate signs, faded backgrounds, or dead bugs on the floor.

Placed carefully in the window were three or four mannequins without heads or arms or legs—just forms on metal stands—wearing housedresses with zippers or buttons up the front—pink and yellow splashed, big-lady torsos.

I always hoped Mama would stop and look; when she didn't I straggled behind and looked over my shoulder. Those housedresses were me grown-up. My head on that body. Someday.

Do I wear housedresses now that I'm all grown-up (and then some)? Not ever. Jeans and sweatshirts or suits and pumps are big-lady garb today. Different dress for women in a different world.

Our lifestyles differ from those of earlier women who were confined mostly to smaller spheres of living—family and neighbors and church and town. Our world has stretched far beyond John Boy's woods. Opportunities to enroll, join, jet, and hire on have sprung up.

Our heads are so full, we rarely have time to reflect and ponder life. We've barely time to *live* it. See ourselves historically? We hardly have time to figure out how we want to change our hairstyles. Jobs and committee chairmanships, plus stints as field-trip chaperones and obligations as Sunday School teachers (or whatever responsibilities are peculiar to us) squeeze our days. Only on a rare getaway (to the beach, perhaps—where we lie in the sun and let our thoughts dip and bob) do we see our lives all-of-a-piece.

I think back to one of those occasions. Under the apple tree in the yard, I write my thoughts down the way Anne Morrow Lindbergh did on her beach vacation described in *Gift from the Sea*. Beside my pad is my Bible, where I look for direction on how to live as a stranger.

I read about Abel, Enoch, Noah, Abraham, and Sarah—"aliens and strangers on earth" (Heb. 11:13).

But I want roots, Lord; we need roots, my family and I. We need a place to be. Is that wrong?

After I think awhile, I decide that it's not. Abraham and Sarah had goods and a place to be—even though it may have been a tent.

A resident foreigner, Lord? I puzzle over the implications.

Then I think of my friends Bill and Christy, who had recently gone overseas to be missionaries to the Muslims. Will they become citizens? Will they adopt Islam? Will they prostrate themselves and pray daily to Mecca? Hardly.

They will honor whatever local customs they can. "I may have to sit on one hand at first to remember not to use it when I eat, because it's important in their culture," Christy told me.

These friends of mine help me see. They're living abroad but carry a sense of rootedness in their hearts. Part of it consists of thinking of parents and children and favorite spots—memories in an internal place to which they can always go. Psychiatrist Viktor Frankl, imprisoned by the Nazis during World War II, says that some prisoners were able to retreat into their inner selves—remembering how life used to be—and live there. Doing so helped preserve their sanity.

Another part of Bill and Christy's rootedness—and ours—is spiritual. In our interior selves, we live rooted in Jesus Christ. While our future home is heaven, our present and spiritual home is the kingdom of God in our spirits, where the Lord Himself lives. He whose feet are like bronze and whose voice is like the sound of rushing waters motivates and directs in ways only the human spirit can hear.

Bill and Christy knew from the start that they were to live as resident foreigners. Our calling to do so came the moment we received Jesus Christ into our lives, and our souls were made sparkling. *You are called to live as resident aliens in this Satan-ruled world.*

How do we learn to live that way as ambassadors in line at the bank, or collectors on our block for the Heart Association? Should we sign up for a supercharged seminar for motivation?

God has provided a better way: "Live by the Spirit" (Gal. 5:16). Live in continuous fellowship with the God who has come into our human spirits and settled down.

In those moments when we do live in Him at the office or supermarket or aerobics class, we know why we're here. Not merely to type fine business letters or find the best grocery bargains or get rid of cellulite. I'm here to stay at home in the Spirit and finish Jesus' work. Every moment I do that, my life will count.

DAY BY DAY WITH GOD

Day 1: Remember how Jesus changed Simon's name to Cephas, or Peter, which means "rock" and signified the kind of person he would become. Decide what name you would like that describes a quality you want to develop. It's OK if the name is unusual. Think of yourself by that name and ask God to cultivate that quality in you. Tell a friend with whom you pray so she can encourage you to continue to cooperate with God.

Day 2: Reflect today on the fact that you are God's ambassador in places where you've been scattered. Name three specific places where you've been scattered and what your ambassadorship means in each.

Day 3: Decide which of the four ways God has outfitted you is most crucial to you: (1) The fact that you've been reborn and indwelled with the Holy Spirit? (2) That you can live confidently instead of pessimistically? (3) That you have an inheritance in heaven, and so your security grows out of your relationship with God? (4) That God is protecting you all the time? Why did you choose what you did?

Day 4: Verse for a woman on the move Memorize 1 Peter 1:8-9 so that your love relationship with God will be central in your mind. Think why you love Him even though you haven't seen Him.

Day 5: Important Compose a one-sentence reminder that expresses your privilege as a resident foreigner who is God's ambassador wherever you are. Copy it on a note card and mount in a place where you will see it, such as on the car dashboard or the bathroom mirror.

BETWEEN FATHER AND DAUGHTER
Daily Prayer Suggestions

Day 1: "As I begin this study, I submit to Your Spirit as my teacher. Illuminate Your Word for me so I may see it from Your perspective."
  Pray also
  ❦ That, as a result, you'll become excited about being a woman sent into the world by God;
  ❦ For specific people you want to influence.

Day 2: "I must remember I'm rooted in You. Teach me to put roots down more deeply in You. One thing that comes to mind is . . . "
  Pray also
  ❦ To see yourself as chosen by God;
  ❦ For a fresh grasp of what it means to be a stranger in this world.

Day 3: "It's easy to take my relationship with You for granted. But when I think about who You are—Lord of the galaxies—I worship You in awe. I do that now."
  Pray also
  ❦ With thanks that God has extended mercy and love to you;
  ❦ For people close to you who need God's mercy and love.

Day 4: "I have a lot to learn about going through trials. Trusting You then can be hard. I choose to let You teach me to do that."
  Pray also
  ❦ For spiritual discernment during trials so that you'll see by faith;
  ❦ To express the joy of Christ while you're in action.

Day 5: "Thank You for Old Testament prophecies about Christ. I am blessed to be living when they have been fulfilled. They're one more way You show Your greatness. I especially appreciate . . . "
  Pray also
  ❦ To deepen your attitude of thankfulness;
  ❦ For chances to talk about prophecy's fulfillment in Christ.

2

CALLED TO BE HOLY AND OBEDIENT
1 Peter 1:13–2:3

❦

YOUR FATHER WRITES

Day 1: Be mentally ready Read 1 Peter 1:13–2:3, then review 1:13.
1. Name three things you do in the morning to prepare yourself for the day. What gets your day off to a bad start? What effect does that have on the rest of the day?

Peter lists three things to do to be ready for the day.
    A. *Prepare your minds for action.* The *King James Version* reads, "Gird up the loins of your mind." What Old Testament event described in Exodus 12:11 might Peter be thinking of?

    Our minds may not be ready for action because they are distracted. What things does Matthew 6:25-34 say we might be preoccupied with? What are we to do about it?

    B. *Be self-controlled.* Or "Be calm and collected in spirit" (Kenneth S. Wuest, *The New Testament: An Expanded Translation*, Grand Rapids: Eerdmans, 1961). Think of a time when you faced a tough day calm and collected, plus a time when you didn't. Write your observations.

    C. *Set your hope fully on the grace to be given you when Jesus Christ is revealed* (1:13). Which of the following definitions of "hope" expresses Peter's meaning—"the feeling or desire that what we want will take place"; or "the confident expectation of something good; Christian optimism"?

2. Our hope is based on God's grace. Which dictionary definition of the word *grace* most nearly expresses what Paul meant by it? In what ways do you most need God's grace during a trial?

Day 2: Be holy Read 1 Peter 1:14-16.

1. By what "family name" does Peter refer to us in verse 14?

It's natural for children to resemble their biological parents and natural for Christians to resemble their Heavenly Father. What does Galatians 2:20 say is the reason? Whom did you resemble before your new birth? In what ways? See Ephesians 2:1-3.

Write a one-sentence portrait of yourself now, according to Ephesians 2:10.

2. What should obedient children of God not do? (1 Peter 1:14)

Write a definition for *conform* by consulting a dictionary, if necessary. Refer also to two or more Bible translations of Romans 12:2.

Reflect on the fact that when we conform to the world, it's as though we're wearing costumes which are designed to fit in the world and which hide our real selves. In truth, who we are outside is to express who we are inside. Who exactly is that, according to John 1:12 and Ephesians 5:8?

3. "Holy," the key word in this chapter, is repeated how many times in verses 15 and 16? What word in 2 Corinthians 6:17 is a syn-

onym? Does that mean we can't associate with non-Christians, according to 1 Corinthians 5:9-10?

What else do you learn about cultivating holiness—or a resemblance to your Father—from 2 Peter 3:18? How does holiness come about?

Complete this sentence: My conclusions about holiness are . . .

Day 3: Appreciate your redemption Read 1 Peter 1:17-21.
1. Recall a time recently when you were extremely afraid. What were the circumstances?

Now recall a recent occasion when you experienced reverential awe of God (for example, you encountered a breathtaking scenic view or some natural wonder or had an answer to prayer). Describe your thoughts and feelings.

The word "fear" in verse 17 has the meaning of reverential awe. Why are we to have that attitude toward God, according to the verse? What's the reason we're to live worshipfully? (vv. 18-20)

2. A key reason to be in awe is that we're *redeemed*. What dictionary definition applies here?

We are to be absolutely convinced of the sacrificial nature of our redemption by God. What word in verse 18 intimates that fact?

Redemption from slavery was priceless to the approximately 60 million slaves in the Roman Empire. A slave could become free if he had enough money to purchase his freedom. Or, sometimes his owner would sell him to someone who would pay the price for his

redemption. Imagine you were a slave then. Why would verses 18
and 19 have special significance to you?

Now imagine you had just learned that your owner purchased your
freedom. How would you feel? What would you say? Apply your
observations to your spiritual redemption.

3. When was Christ chosen to pay the price for our redemption?
What does Paul say was the reason? (See Ephesians 1:4-5.) Read
1 Peter 1:21 in another translation and write the central thought.

Write a note of praise and thanks to your Lord and master for
purchasing your spiritual freedom. In what ways are you free? Why
was He the only one who could accomplish this? How does the
fact that you are free affect your daily life?

Day 4: The living Word of God Read 1 Peter 1:22-25.
1. Which do you prefer: a bath or a shower? Describe how you feel
when you step out and towel off.

First Peter 1:22 says you are cleansed spiritually. How does that
takes place? How does Psalm 119:9 say you can stay clean?

2. A quality that obedient Christians demonstrate is love. Peter uses
two different Greek words for "love" in verse 22. The first means
"brotherly kindness" (or "sisterly kindness," for that matter). To
understand it, think of what that term implies and of a person for
whom you have that kind of love. Describe your relationship.

The second kind of love is deep, heartfelt, and sacrificial. Think of one time when someone demonstrated this kind of love toward you. What was its effect? Where does that love come from? (See Rom. 5:5.) What words in 1 Peter 1:23 shed more light on why we are able to love that way?

3. The Word of God, through which He brings about our personal transformation, is described as imperishable. How would you describe something that is imperishable? Do you own anything except your Bible like that? Think about how unique your Bible is among all your possessions. What can it do for you?

Day 5: Maintain a healthy appetite Read 1 Peter 2:1-3.
1. When you're busy, what junk food are you most tempted to grab instead of eating a nourishing meal?

   Five things in verse 1 are like junk food because they kill our appetite for the Word of God. List them here and personalize a dictionary definition to fit each of them. What words in that verse tell you to rid yourself completely of each one?

2. What is there about a baby's reaction to hunger that makes it a perfect example in verse 2? How does your hunger for Scripture compare to that?

   To further understand the deep longing we're to have for the Scriptures, describe a craving you've had for a favorite food. How does your craving for God's Word compare to that? What does verse 2 say will happen if we continue to ingest the Word of God and obey it?

Would you think of mixing soda pop with milk in a newborn baby's bottle? With that in mind, what do you think is Peter's main point in verse 2?

Reread verse 3 and think of a time when you experienced God's goodness. Describe the event, plus your thoughts and feelings.

REFLECTIONS ALONG THE WAY

Words have given me a lot of trouble. That's because I assign such precise meanings to them. Take *holy* for example. To me it meant "pure, without sin." That definition posed a big problem, however; if God was calling me to be pure and perfect, I was in trouble. There is no way I could achieve holiness.

As I saw it, my only choice was to pretend to be grown-up the way I had when I was a child and wore big-lady shoes and trailing skirts. The costume I fashioned was a careful copy of my mental image of Mrs. Perfect Christian. My costume concealed the flaws hidden beneath, the way the best-tailored clothes are designed to.

I lingered in Christian childhood, playing "let's pretend" far too long; but finally, I did begin to grow up. That brought with it an urgent desire to make my outer demeanor reflect my reborn inner nature. By then I knew that God doesn't expect us to be perfect, and that my interpretations had come through a perfectionist's mind-set. So I reexamined the biblical teaching of holiness.

The word *holiness* itself held the key. "It signifies separation to God" and "the conduct befitting those so separate" (W.E. Vine, *Vine's Expository Dictionary of Old and New Testament Words*, New Tappan, N.J.: Fleming H. Revell Co., 1981).

I think of the head-joined Siamese twins separated by neurosurgeon Benjamin Carson, a feat never before accomplished. Babies Patrick and Benjamin Binder had separate brains but shared crucial veins at the back of the head. These had to be untangled and reconstructed in order for the brothers to be separated ("Divided for Life," Bob Chuvala, *Christian Herald*, April 1988, pp. 14–18).

God had to perform an even more delicate surgery in our inner woman. "God used His surgical knife to cut the believing sinner loose from his evil nature" (Kenneth S. Wuest, *Word Studies in the Greek*

New Testament, Romans, Vol. I, Grand Rapids: Eerdmans, 1955, p. 93). The potential for that corrective surgery to take place in us came about because He chose to send Jesus Christ to pay for our sins. The surgery itself actually takes place the moment we receive Christ as Savior.

That spiritual surgery took place for me the Sunday evening in Flushing, New York when I knelt at my bedside. "God, I have to know if it's true. If Jesus Christ is real, if He is divine, if I can know Him—then I want to."

Without understanding, I knew Jesus Christ was the Son of God. He had established a personal relationship with me. That moment I had become somehow different, and I knew it absolutely.

Until the moment of new birth, the person who is Marion had been inexorably joined to her old nature just as the Binder twins were joined at the head. That old nature is the one that had controlled me since the time of my first temper tantrum. Only God Almighty could accomplish separation and gift me with His own perfect nature, and He did that at the moment of my conversion.

Separation had already been accomplished for me! My responsibility was to keep choosing to live in the sparkling, new nature God had provided, internalizing and obeying His written Word.

Even though I know that, obedience certainly isn't always a cinch. That's because He didn't toss my old self-centered nature into Gehenna. The Marion-centered nature that wanted to be praised and petted was alive and well in me. Now, though, I no longer had to wear it as if it were all I owned. I was free to choose the nature in which I would live.

Doing so has been harder since my husband Jack and I left full-time Christian service for life in the mainstream of secular society. During the years I was a stateside missionary, it was as though I wore an invisible name tag: *Preacher's wife. Tell her no dirty jokes. Don't share the latest gossip with her. Extend no invitations to parties where we let our hair down.*

When I was no longer the preacher's missus, I wore no invisible name tag, no protective shield. No one protected me from four-letter words. This is more of a test of how authentic my Christianity is than were my earlier years. Am I up to it?

No, but Jesus Christ, who wore no invisible shield Himself when He was in the world, is up to it. I'm learning to count on His presence, through the person of the Holy Spirit, day by day.

DAY BY DAY WITH GOD

Day 1: **List things you can do** to become more calmer, cooler, and more collected. How can you make these changes permanent?

Day 2: **Take time today** to look in your spiritual mirror. What quality of Jesus Christ do you most need to cultivate? In what ways would it improve your life? Write that quality on a piece of paper and put it on the refrigerator as a daily reminder.

Day 3: **Verses for a woman on the move** Copy 1 Peter 1:18-19 on a note card and start to memorize it. As you do so, think about how valuable you must be to God, for He sacrificed His only Son for you! Think too about how valuable the men, women, and children you see every day—who barely acknowledge His existence—are to Him.

Day 4: **Promise yourself** that today, you'll think of one person whom you only pretend to love. Then write down one way to begin practicing genuine love toward him or her. Hold yourself accountable before God to do it.

Day 5: **Evaluate** your spiritual eating habits. How does my spiritual appetite compare to earlier days? If it is sluggish, why? Am I starving, snacking, or eating solid and regular meals? What physical shape would I be in if I ate good food the way I internalized the Word of God? If I really do want to grow up in my salvation, what one change must I make? When will I begin doing that and how? Talk over the subject with someone who will check on your progress.

BETWEEN FATHER AND DAUGHTER
Daily Prayer Suggestions

Day 1: "Father, I commit myself to spend time with You every morning so that I'll be prepared for the day. In order to do that, I'll pledge to . . . "

Pray also
❧ For strength and wisdom to handle interruptions;
❧ To live more expectantly because God is in your life.

Day 2: "The idea of being holy scares me because I know how weak I am. How I thank You now that the ability to be holy comes from You."

Pray also

❧ For honesty about problem areas in your life;

❧ For help to conform more nearly to Christ in those areas.

Day 3: "Instead of going through life without even seeing things that show Your wonder, I want to fully appreciate You through them. I'll begin by . . . "

Pray also

❧ Reflecting on the cost and result of God's redemption of you;

❧ To see yourself as a slave to God in your corner of the world.

Day 4: "Loving some people deeply doesn't come easily. To be the woman You want to be, though, I need to learn how. Use the situations in my life to teach me. One obstacle to learning I see is . . . "

Pray also

❧ For help in turning over to God a relationship with an individual who is difficult to love;

❧ To be so committed to Christ that you'll want to be obedient.

Day 5: "My spiritual appetite for Your Word isn't always what it should be. Show me the things that spoil my appetite. I want to be as hungry as a baby is for her bottle."

Pray also

❧ For insight as to how you need to grow up in Christ;

❧ To be so convinced that the Lord is good that it becomes natural to talk about His goodness.

3

CHOSEN TO BE LIVING WITNESSES
1 Peter 2:4-12

❦

YOUR FATHER WRITES

Day 1: Come to the living Stone Read 1 Peter 2:4-12; then review verse 4.

1. As with human relationships, the one we have with Christ begins when a personal meeting takes place. How does that personal meeting take place, according to John 1:12 and 3:16-17? Describe the occasion when your relationship with Him began. Or tell why you can say today, "I know Christ personally."

2. Jesus is called the "living Stone" in verse 4. To understand that term, think of the most valuable gemstone you own and tell briefly why it's important to you. Why is Jesus called the "living Stone"? What insight do you gain from 1 Peter 1:3; John 1:4; and 5:26?

3. Jesus described Himself and His ministry in various ways. What names did He give Himself in these verses, and what do they reveal of His nature and ministry to us?

	Name	Nature	Ministry
John 6:35			
John 10:7-9			
John 15:1-3			

What word in 1 John 1:3-4 describes the day-by-day relationship Christ wants to have with us? What dictionary definition helps you better understand what should take place? Compare a relationship you have with a close friend to the one you have with the Lord. What conclusions do you reach?

Day 2: We are living stones Read 1 Peter 2:5-6.
1. Imagine that you've been commissioned to plan a building in which God Himself is going to live. What material would you choose for outer walls? Inner walls? What fabrics for the interior? What would be the main requirements for the priests who would serve in it? What do your choices imply about that building?

Christians are called "living stones" in verse 5. From where do we obtain our life? (1 John 5:11-12) What kind of life is it? How does it differ from the life with which we were born?

We're being built up into a spiritual house (v. 5). Another term used in the New Testament is "one body" (Rom. 12:5). What in Ephesians 2:22 seems most important to remember about our becoming a dwelling for God?

2. What kind of priesthood does God call us to join? (1 Peter 2:5) From what you learned in study 2, how would you define the term *priesthood*?

What tribe of Israel was assigned the duty of priest in the Old Testament? (Num. 3:6-9) What was their job? (Num. 8:19) Who else were called to be priests—not in the temple, but in everyday life? (Ex. 19:3-6) Why? (Rev. 1:6) Read 1 Peter 2:5 again, putting your name in it. Write down your questions and reflections.

Keep in mind that a priest was one who could approach God, while others could not. What additional insight does that give about the ministry to which you're called?

The priests' primary function was to offer animal sacrifices for the people's sins. What parallel responsibility is assigned Christians? (1 Peter 2:5) These sacrifices are not lambs that we place on the altar to atone for sin, but unselfish acts we perform out of love for God. What are some of those activities, according to Romans 12:1; 2 Corinthians 8:5; Philippians 4:18; and Hebrews 13:15-16?

3. Imagine you were picking out a cornerstone for the building you were erecting. What prerequisites would you have in mind? Who is God's cornerstone? (See Acts 4:8-12.) What words are used in 1 Peter 2:6 to describe Him?

Read Ephesians 2:19-22 and draw a picture of the spiritual building Paul describes. Name the cornerstone. Then name those who are part of the foundation. Then add living stones—like yourself, if you are a Christian, and other women you know. Write names on the stones. Now, imagine the building complete, with saints from throughout the world and all the ages. Write your response in the form of a prayer.

Day 3: The cornerstone becomes a stumbling block Read 1 Peter 2:7-8.
1. Describe a time when you tripped and fell. How did you respond to the fact that something got in your way—even though it may

have been something that belonged there, like a curb?

Some people "tripped" over Jesus while others accepted Him as the cornerstone of the church. What phrases in 1 Peter 2:7-8 describe these two groups?

Read Mark 6:1-3 and John 8:42-59 — situations in which groups of people rejected Jesus. Choose one and rewrite the account in your own words. Include your thoughts on the subject.

2. For those who believe, Jesus is the one who provides salvation from sin plus eternal life. For those who reject Him, He becomes Judge. Read 1 Corinthians 1:18-25 and sum up what the passage says about the world's kind of wisdom. What is the message the world disobeys? (1 Peter 3:18)

Every individual who rejects Christ is destined for punishment, infers Peter in 2:8. Take a few minutes to think of friends who fall into that category. Tell God that you want Him to use you to show them that He is worthy of their trust.

3. Read Matthew 9:36 again. What was Jesus' attitude toward the unsaved? Can you think of ways in which your attitude toward this group in your world needs to become more like His?

Day 4: Seeing ourselves differently Read 1 Peter 2:9-12.
1. In contrast to unbelievers in verse 8, Peter uses four terms in verse 9 to describe who we are as Christians.
    ❦ A *chosen people.* Who does Exodus 6:6-8 say were God's original chosen people? What promises does God make in that

passage that are true for you? According to Deuteronomy 7:7-8, why did He choose them—and by implication, us?

❦ A *royal priesthood.* Reflect on the following facts about the Old Testament priesthood. (1) The Levites, the priestly tribe, were given no land in Canaan. God was their inheritance. (2) They were consecrated to God and were to remain pure from defilement. (3) They served God in the temple. What do you think these facts imply for Christian women today?

❦ A *holy nation.* What action are we specifically forbidden to perform, according to Exodus 20:4? How do you think that applies to Christians today?

❦ A *people belonging to God.* Name a valuable possession you own. What rights over it do you have as a result? What insight does that give as to God's rights in your life?

According to 2:9, our responsibility is to "declare the praises of Him who called you out of darkness into His wonderful light." The thought behind that statement is that "each citizen of heaven is a living 'advertisement' for the virtues of God and the blessings of the Christian life" (Warren Wiersbe, *The Bible Exposition Commentary,* Vol. 2, Wheaton, Ill.: Victor Books, 1989, p. 402). Write some advertising copy describing the qualities of God and the reasons why people should want to become Christians. Brainstorm some ways you can be a living advertisement for God in the place where you spend the most time.

2. What is the key word in verse 10b? How does the dictionary define it? What statements in Romans 5:6-8 amplify Peter's point?

Imagine yourself as a condemned prisoner, standing in court and pleading for leniency. Then, based on Psalm 106:1-2, write out your expression of thanksgiving for God's deliverance from the penalty of sin.

Day 5: Keep on keeping on Read 1 Peter 2:11-12.

1. What fictional character from a book, play, or TV would you describe as a "good" woman? Why? Does she seem human, or is she idealistically portrayed?

Do you think you are ever too hard on yourself as a Christian, expecting too much of yourself? Imagine you're telling a friend about a time when you recently did that. What would you say?

To live good lives, we must keep seeing ourselves as strangers in this world. Why? We must also "abstain from sinful desires" (v. 11). To abstain means "to hold yourself constantly back from something." What particular strong desire, or lust, do you find yourself struggling with most? What help does Galatians 5:16-26 provide?

2. "Live such good lives among the pagans that, though they accuse you of doing wrong, they may see your good deeds and glorify God on the day He visits us," states verse 12. What kinds of acts within your power to perform could be called "good deeds"? In addition to the help they provide, what other benefit are they?

Have you ever been accused of doing wrong, even though you hadn't? What were the circumstances? Would you respond differently if you had it to do over? If so, how would you respond?

"The separated life of a Christian is one of the most powerful means God has of convicting the world of its sin" (*Wuest's Word Studies*, Vol. II, p. 60). What person do you know who has lived that way? How has he or she been a godly influence?

REFLECTIONS ALONG THE WAY

A priest? Who, me?

I just couldn't relate to the idea, maybe because women priests haven't been a part of my experience.

Since I *knew* that God lived in me, it has been much easier for me to grasp the idea of being a temple. God's Word repeatedly insisted that was true. "Don't you know that you yourselves are God's temple and that God's Spirit lives in you?" (1 Cor. 3:16) Besides, I'd sensed Him in me and had been taught by Him.

On days when I was spiritually sensitive, the idea of being God's house made me gasp and examine my soul for spots and stains. *Is my temple clean enough for God to live in?* Of course not. No matter how scrupulous I might be, my cleansing is still an act of His grace.

When I thought deeply about the subject, I wondered exactly how I was to live this idea out. *How am I to be a temple on Monday morning at 8 o'clock?*

When I related it to the familiar (mobile army surgical hospitals— M.A.S.H. units), the answer became apparent. These tent hospitals had to remain as free of dirt and grime as possible in locales where they were set up. Their role at the battlefront was that of healing facilities. The surgeons who operated in them were to be committed to that practice.

A mobile temple. That's what I am.

But my mind was ready to take the analogy further. *Like the surgeons in those hospitals, I am also a priest called to minister.* Then I stopped frowning inwardly at the idea. *Gender doesn't matter here.*

Male and female, our job description is the same—to offer spiritual sacrifices and attend to the "wounded" in the office, the beauty shop, at PTA, art guild, exercise class, and wherever they are found.

Such an overwhelming responsibility. How can I manage it? By being filled with the Spirit every day—and, therefore, empowered and led by Him. It's His ministry, but He'll use my past experiences so I can empathize; my emotional nature so I can cry and rejoice with my fellow women; my possessions so I can help fill needs.

Yes, we are called to be a mobile priesthood. The women I admire the most, I realized, are taking part. Sherry, a friend with serious health problems of her own, is ministering to wounded people in her apartment complex.

Quietly friendly, she makes sure to become acquainted with other women who are folding sheets next to her in the laundry room and offers them invitations to her apartment for tea.

One of the women whom Sherry has gotten to know well that way is a recently divorced young woman who is confused and feels like a failure. Sherry's quiet, loving words and introduction to God are exactly what she needs.

Patricia, another friend of mine, has been offering spiritual sacrifices to God by helping an elderly neighbor no longer able to care for herself. When it became plain that the woman could no longer live at home, Pat kept coming to her friend's bedside, speaking reassuringly to the woman's panic and soothing her with reminders of Jesus' love during her transition to a nursing home.

One thing strikes me about Sherry and Patricia and myself: *we are such ordinary women.* But then, humanly speaking, the incarnated Jesus was such an ordinary man.

The world needs priests who are ordinary women. From where will they come except our kitchens and bedrooms? They certainly won't appear like a legion of angels from heaven. Their ranks will only be formed as people like me step forward and take our places. A priesthood in regal robes lined up silent and immobile simply won't do.

God's plan is to use ordinary women who have Him living in their spirits to offer spiritual sacrifices and tend wounds in this world. Experience tells me that the needy are everywhere: in shopping malls, classrooms, hospitals, housing developments. Is the woman sitting next to me at the bus stop one of them? My stoolmate at the lunch counter?

But I know how tough it can be to minister consistently. My

failures provide me a clue. I shrink back when my own spiritual life is in disarray—when I am too preoccupied with my own wounded ego to think of others.

M.A.S.H. surgeons come to mind again. They may have been tired and disgruntled; still their commitment to offer whatever healing was in their power took priority. The answer for us priests? Always the same: Live in the Spirit and keep aligning our lives to that of our Lord.

I think of the times I've overcome my natural resistance and obeyed the Holy Spirit's directive to offer a spiritual sacrifice here or offer salve for a wound there. I relive the unparalleled sense of fulfillment it brings. Without a doubt, that's the only motivation any of us needs.

DAY BY DAY WITH GOD

Day 1: Important Instead of just going over troubling events in your mind, begin to come to God continually during your day through conversational prayer about them. Make a note of specific ways doing that changes your response when trouble hits.

Day 2: Ask God to show you how you can begin helping a woman or girl who's hurting in some way. God will answer your prayer. Keep an account of what happens.

Day 3: Prepare now to answer someone who says, "My religion is to obey the Ten Commandments." Plan to tell how you had similar thoughts (if this is the case) and how you learned differently. Or tell about the experience of someone close to you. Make notes now of what you would say.

Day 4: Verse for a woman on the move Commit 1 Peter 2:9 to memory in the translation that most hits home for you. After you've learned it, personalize it by putting in your name and saying it to yourself as a reminder each morning while you're in the bathroom.

Day 5: Get serious with God It's time to give Him the habit that keeps you feeling guilty. Picture that habit as an item you're giving away and will never reclaim. Vow to lean on the Holy Spirit and persist no matter what. Write out and date your request. Why not make yourself accountable to another Christian to see this through?

BETWEEN FATHER AND DAUGHTER
Daily Prayer Suggestions

Day 1: "You're alive, Jesus. I can't comprehend all the implications of that, but I want to stop now and reflect on ones You show me."
Pray also
❦ For more appreciation of Christ as the one who brought the church into being;
❦ Reflecting on the ways He is to be honored in your church.

Day 2: "To live my life at work, in my community, and in my church more aware of Your life in me—that's what will make the difference. What renovations will that call for?"
Pray also
❦ To see yourself as a spiritual sacrifice, to give more unselfishly;
❦ For others you know who are living stones in God's temple.

Day 3: "I pray for those around me who trip over Jesus all the time."
Pray also
❦ To see these people through God's eyes;
❦ To become aware of opportunities to show and tell who Jesus is.

Day 4: "We Christian women have been chosen by You to be Christ to the world. What's one way I can do that?"
Pray also
❦ To see yourself as completely owned by God;
❦ Reflecting on the power of the Holy Spirit to enable you.

Day 5: "You know the lusts I struggle with and how discouraged I get. I'm so glad You haven't given up on me. As I meditate in Your presence, show me how I can overcome them by living in the Spirit."
Pray also
❦ To grow stronger in your ability to choose to do God's will;
❦ That false accusations made against you may be used for good.

4

CITIZENS AND WORKERS
1 Peter 2:13-25

YOUR FATHER WRITES

Day 1: Submission to governmental authority Read 1 Peter 2:13-25, then review 13-15.

1. Imagine you're taking a night class at a local Bible college entitled "The Christian as a Citizen." What questions will you pose in an initial discussion as those that bother you most?

The key word in this section is "submit." What one-word dictionary definition seems most appropriate? Review passages in which submission is taught (1 Peter 2:13, 18; 3:1). Does it imply that we are to do so once or continually? Do you meet difficulties in fulfilling 2:13-15 in your personal life? What are they?

2. According to verse 13, why should we submit to governmental authority? What further insight do you gain from Romans 13:1-5?

The "king," or the highest office in the land, corresponds to what position in our government? The governor, or those who enforce the law and mete out punishment, remind you of whom?

You've been asked to write a paper stating your position on the responsibility of a Christian as a citizen. Put down some notes, glean 1 Peter 1-2 for information, and include your response to the following quote: "A true Christian submits himself to author-

ity because he is first of all submitted to Christ" (Wiersbe, *The Bible Exposition Commentary*, Vol. 2, p. 405).

3. The second reason for being a good citizen is described in verse 15. What is it? Sometimes, however, Christians cannot obey governmental authorities. Peter and John were in that situation when they were arrested for preaching the Good News and warned not to do so again. Write the answer they gave Jewish leaders in your own words for your class paper. (See Acts 4:19-20.)

Day 2: Citizens as servants Read 1 Peter 2:16-17.
1. Under what circumstances do you feel freest? Look up "freedom" in the dictionary; then write a personal definition.

2. The word translated "servants" (literally, "slaves") means "one who is in subjection." Think of times when you have subordinated your personal freedom for the sake of someone else. What insight does that give regarding Christian citizenship? Name the numerous ways in which you can fulfill your responsibility as a Christian citizen.

3. Peter begins and ends 2:13-18 with general directives. Read them and write a one-sentence summary to put in your paper of what he says. What part do the four verbs in verse 17 play?

Explain the difference between honoring the position of a government officer and endorsing his policy. Suppose the President (or Prime Minister) had just spoken on TV about a new policy with which you disagreed. What would be a respectful way to say what you thought?

Day 3: Christian employees Read 1 Peter 2:18-20.

1. Recall the job in which you had problems because of unfair employment practices, or think of someone else's work experience. Describe the problem and how it affected you or the other person. How was it resolved, if at all?

What verb used in verse 18 was used in verse 13? The word for "slave" here means "household servant." It included domestics and those holding a wide variety of jobs. In what ways do you identify? Employers are comparable to "masters." Refer to Ephesians 6:9 and Colossians 4:1; then write the kind of statement you'd read at a convention of Christian employers entitled "Managing Your Employees the Biblical Way."

2. Look up *respect* in the dictionary and brainstorm ways you could show respect to a difficult employer. Suppose you are writing a "Christian Employee Manual." After you read these Scriptures, list in the manual ways God wants a Christian employee to behave:
   - Ecclesiastes 9:10
   - Ephesians 6:5-8
   - Colossians 3:22-25
   - 1 Timothy 6:1
   - Titus 2:9-10

3. Read verses 19 and 20 in an alternate translation. While it isn't legal today for an employer to beat a worker, how would you phrase it for inclusion in the Christian Employee Manual?

Paraphrase other principles to include from Luke 6:32-34 and Romans 12:17-21. Reflect before God on the last sentence of 1 Peter 2:20 and make it your prayer.

Day 4: Following Christ's example Read 1 Peter 2:21-23.

1. Think of a time when you chose to suffer because of someone else's mistreatment. What did you learn from that experience?

   To what principle in verse 20 does Peter refer in verse 21? What man or woman comes to mind as a role model for you of that principle? In what ways was he or she an example to you?

2. Do you sometimes feel unable to relate to Jesus as a role model when you work? Read Mark 6:1-3. What phrase in verse 3 provides help? Write your thoughts.

   Verse 22 is a quote of Isaiah's prophecy (Isa. 53:9). What qualities of Jesus foretold in Isaiah 53:7-9 are appropriate for us to practice as workers? For inclusion in your Christian Employee Manual, tell how Bible writers say we can do that:
   - Isaiah 41:10
   - John 15:4
   - Philippians 4:13

3. What alternative behavior to demanding one's rights is described here? How does Jesus demonstrate that behavior on the cross? (See Luke 23:34.)

   Sort out your thoughts about being a Christian worker. What is to be your number one priority? In what ways can you impact those with whom and for whom you work? Can you always, therefore, demand your rights?

Day 5: Because of Christ's death and resurrection Read 1 Peter 2:24-25.

1. When was the first time that the message "Christ died for your sins" had an impact on you? Why do you think Peter reminds his

readers of Christ's substitutionary death here? What does it have to do with citizenship and submission at work?

What gift that is now yours as a result of Christ's death do you depend on most? Imagine you're telling a coworker how that gift changed your life. What would you say?

2. Reflect on the first phrase in verse 24, "He Himself bore our sins in His body on the tree"; then write your thoughts on its significance, taking into account the central message of John 10:30 and 14:7-9. Now read the first phrase in verse 24 aloud. Which words do you emphasize and why?

To be "dead to sin" means to be "separated from sin." That took place when we received Christ as Savior and, at the same time, identified with His death for us. So, we have a new nature and can live rightly. How can that make us more productive in our work?

3. Jesus is your Shepherd (v. 25). How does knowing that enable you to be a better citizen and worker? Expand your concept of Christ's protection and participation in your life as you work and as you are active in community affairs.

REFLECTIONS ALONG THE WAY

As a working Christian woman, I've felt dichotomized. From every newsstand I pass, slick magazines with feminine genderisms in the titles and female CEOs on the covers insist: *Be tough-minded. Look out for number one if you want to make it to the top.*

But from Peter and his peers I hear a philosophy that sounds, with its gentleness, like soft organ music: *Marion, I want you to be a servant where you work.*

Does Peter mean for me to bow like a geisha and back off? Does the New Testament mean for me to smile passively when I'm taken advantage of in the workplace? Like the time an employer explained why a male employee earned more than me for doing the same work with, "A man needs more."

I rebel. It's not fair for me to always have to acquiesce. I'd feel pale and bland and stunted. I recoil at the idea of never standing up for myself when a boss is more demanding than a two-year-old. *How can Peter's high-minded philosophy work in a world where companies look hungrily for patsies they can take advantage of?*

Anyway, do Peter's words really apply today? Slaves in the Roman Empire had no wage and hour boards, no unions, no laws against sexual harassment and discrimination. Women in today's work force *are* protected in many respects by law. Am I supposed to waive my rights and meekly take whatever's handed me?

At one time, living that way was the norm for me because I saw myself as a doormat. But at midlife, by the grace of God, that changed—not with the whisk of a wand but gradually, as God introduced me to my real self, a woman whom He loved and treasured. As I felt myself growing into a real person, I became able to speak up. *Wait a minute; that contract isn't fair.*

Since I wasn't meant to be a doormat, I needed to know a healthy response to the teaching of servanthood. Insight came at a celebration time in my life—the birth of twin grandsons. It seemed appropriate that the coming-to-see about servanthood coincided with the changing of diapers.

What I saw was this: I'd supposed, to that point, that I was called to be a servant to mankind—in this case, to every obstreperous human for whom I worked. *But that's wrong, Marion. Absolutely wrong.*

I was called to serve, all right. But whom?

The Lord God Almighty! Did I not enter His employ the moment I was born into His kingdom?

I opened my eyes wider and smiled down in my newfound understanding at the baby I held. *I have only one Master,* I told the infant in my mind. *God may lead me to work behind a counter, a word processor as a free-lance writer, or as a homemaker. But wherever, He is the master I serve.*

Looking back over my working life, I realize that I've viewed my employers mostly as good bosses (friendly, easy to get along with, fair) or bad bosses (distant, demanding, unfair). But my focus has been on the wrong person. It should have been on the Lord. In His name and power, I'm to move in my workplace to fulfill His purposes.

In order to serve God, Jesus served man. As He arose every morning to hammer or to preach, service was His single goal. Not to prostrate Himself in subservience to everyone else, but to assume daily the position of servanthood that the Father showed Him.

At the same time, Jesus was confrontive in love. To imitate Him may be part of our own ministry of servanthood. Sometimes, we may even have to refuse to obey orders, like the time I was asked by an employer to lie to customers. After praying for guidance, I nervously told my employer, "I'm sorry. I can't follow those instructions," and explained why.

My superior paused and stared at me. "OK. Do it your way. But it had better not cause problems in the business." It didn't.

I realized that Jesus had a higher purpose than to become the best-known carpenter in Nazareth or the most sought-after evangelist in Palestine. And every woman who is a member of His body on earth right now shares His higher purpose.

Certainly, if we work, we should receive a fair wage. Certainly we want positions that best use our skills. It may even be His will for us to achieve great success. But we are to allow the Lord Christ to decide where we are to serve and what our goals are to be.

Some women I know have acted as servants in dramatic ways. One friend believed she should refuse a promotion offered her and suggest it be given to the perfectly capable fellow employee with seniority who had been passed over. That's what she did, saying, "I didn't need the extra money as much as the other woman."

Another friend allowed an insecure supervisor to take credit for her ideas on company improvement.

Are we always to make sacrifices like these? Not necessarily. How do we know? "I will send to you from the Father the Spirit of truth" (John 15:26).

Does living as a servant require sacrifice? Of course. "If any woman would come after Me, she must deny herself and take up her cross and follow Me" (Mark 8:34, personal translation).

Does servanthood require inseparable, ongoing, branch-in-vine union? Absolutely. "If a woman remains in Me and I in her, she will bear much fruit; apart from Me you can do nothing" (John 15:5, personal translation).

Can a woman be Salesperson of the Year and still be a servant?

Entirely possible. But when she can't be both, the choice to make is clear.

I looked down at the baby again, now asleep in my arms. *Servanthood. In whatever ways God directs.* Why did I think that, of necessity, the term had a negative connotation? Another myth debunked. I ran my finger across the baby's fuzzy head and wiped milk from his chin. *Becoming a servant at work could turn out to be some of the richest times of my life.*

DAY BY DAY WITH GOD

Day 1: Do a self-evaluation How law-abiding and respectful of civil authorities are you? Do you honor a person's position even though you may dislike his political action? Monitor your conversation and actions this week and note any discrepancies. Evaluate with a family member, group member, or friend any changes you need to make within yourself.

Day 2: Verse for a woman on the move As you memorize 1 Peter 2:24, meditate on what each phrase means and visualize how you'll live it out.

Day 3: Before breakfast, ask the Holy Spirit to make you aware today of how respectfully you respond to those for whom or with whom you work—at home or outside. Before bedtime, decide specifically what changes you need to make and write a reminder here. Do you need to make yourself accountable to someone for this in order to follow through?

Day 4: Do it today Which person in your workday frustrates you most? Are you making matters worse? If so, how? What one thing can you do about it *now*?

Day 5: To motivate yourself, put up a sign someplace where you work: "Sheep follow the Shepherd." You will know that means you are to follow Jesus in servanthood. Keep a record here of times during the day when the sign influences you to respond in a godlier way than you wanted to at first.

BETWEEN FATHER AND DAUGHTER
Daily Prayer Suggestions

Day 1: "I confess that I haven't always respected government officials' positions, partly because I disagree with their politics. Forgive me, Lord. Teach me balance in this area."
Pray also
❧ That corrupt officials will be convicted of sin and, when necessary, removed from office;
❧ For those officials you know who are Christians.

Day 2: "As I consider the way I fulfill my responsibility as a Christian citizen, You are teaching me that . . . "
Pray also
❧ Committing yourself to make changes in one needy area now;
❧ For godly people to influence our political system.

Day 3: "I get tired of domestic chores and complain about them. That would change if I did them in union with You, reflecting on Your presence as I dust or clean the bathroom. Not just in housework either, but in other ways, such as . . . "
Pray also
❧ For a cooperative spirit with God as He works changes in you;
❧ That this positive attitude will spread to all areas of your life.

Day 4: "The Son of God, by whom all things were created, actually stood silent when He was maligned and abused by us mortals. I worship You now as I think about that."
Pray also
❧ To be less retaliatory in a certain relationship;
❧ For God to sensitize you to times when you demand your rights.

Day 5: "Thank You, Father, for sending Your Son to be my substitute. I need to keep that central in my mind as I work. If I do, good things will happen, namely . . . "
Pray also
❧ With gratitude for the specific gifts that are yours because of Christ;
❧ Committing yourself to follow Christ by living righteously in a significant way related to your work.

5

MAKING LIFE COUNT
IN FAMILY RELATIONSHIPS
1 Peter 3:1-7

YOUR FATHER WRITES

Day 1: Don't preach it — live it Read 1 Peter 3:1-7; then review verses 1-2.

1. Complete these sentences:
- ❦ I blow up at my family when . . .
- ❦ The reasons this usually happens are . . .
- ❦ What I'd like to do then is . . .

One particular time when family relationships become unpleasant is when Christian wives preach to their non-Christian husbands. What advice (also applicable in other family situations) is given here? What additional insight do you gain from Galatians 6:9?

2. The key word in 1 Peter 3:1 is "submissive." What does it mean? What verbs in 2:17 help explain it?

Is only the wife to submit, or does the teaching have broader applications? (Eph. 5:21) What does it mean regarding the forming and expressing of your own opinions? If you were speaking to the women in your church on submission, what would you say?

3. Two qualities Peter mentions here that tend to influence people to consider Christ are purity and reverence. Consider the first quality, purity. What is Peter's answer in 2 Peter 1:3 to our struggle to be pure? What further ideas do you find in 1 John 1:8-9? Write instructions for yourself based on what you read.

The second quality is reverence. Reflect on the second part of verse 2 in *The Amplified Bible* and think of two ways you can put the principle stated there into practice with your mate or other family members. That version says *revere* is "to honor, esteem (appreciate, prize), and [in the human sense] adore him; [and adore means] to admire, praise, be devoted to, deeply love and enjoy [your husband]."

Day 2: Be beautiful Read 1 Peter 3:3-4.
1. Look up *beautiful* in the dictionary; then describe a beautiful woman. What does the word "adornment" ("ornament" in the *King James Version*) mean?

Which of the following statements is true?
   ❦ Peter says women shouldn't wear adornments at all.
   ❦ Peter says women shouldn't rely on adornments for beauty.

2. Manners of dress change with the times. What examples of that do you see in Genesis 24:65; Isaiah 3:16, 18-23? Name the three ways of adorning oneself mentioned in 1 Peter 3:3.

After reading 3:3 in an alternate translation, tell what kind of dress you think is out of place for a Christian woman today. Give two reasons to avoid the kind of dress Peter is talking about.

3. In verse 4, Peter advises us to dress from the inside out. Read Colossians 3:12 and 1 Timothy 2:9-10 and list the qualities with which we are to clothe ourselves.

First Peter 3:4 teaches that women are to acquire "a gentle and quiet spirit." How does Colossians 3:15-17 say we can achieve inner tranquility? What does that mean to you?

Would you like to revise or add to your description of a beautiful woman? How?

Day 3: Historical role models Read 1 Peter 3:5a.

1. What Old Testament woman do you most admire? What quality of hers makes her attractive to you?

The women you are to emulate are called "holy." Review lesson 2 and explain what that means.

The women of old described in 1 Peter 3:5a "put their hope in God." Which definition of "hope" do you think applies?
  🐾 "A wish that something would happen"
  🐾 "A confident expectation that something will happen"

2. Identify the women written about below, the situations they found themselves in, the actions they took, and the character qualities they needed in order to act.

	Identity	Situation	Action	Quality
Exodus 1:15-16				
Exodus 2:1-10				
Ruth 1:3-18				
Luke 1:26-38				

Despite tough family circumstances, these women made their lives count. Choose the woman with whom you identify most and imagine she lived next door. Tell about her experience as though it were happening now.

3. Think of a current difficult situation in your family. What quality demonstrated by one of the women in the chart above or described elsewhere in this lesson do you need? Ask God how else that woman's life can be a model. Write what He shows you.

Day 4: Learning from Sarah Read 1 Peter 3:5-6.

1. Imagine you've been asked to give Sarah an award. What would you say in your presentation speech?

   Sarah called her husband "master." What appropriate modern word would you substitute? Paraphrase *The Amplified Bible* version of 3:6a below, putting it in the present tense and inserting your name and that of your mate. "Sarah obeyed Abraham (following his guidance and acknowledging his headship over her) by calling him lord—master, leader, authority." (If single, begin "A woman is to obey her husband. . . . ") How would you define *headship*?

2. Was Sarah right in submitting to Abraham in Genesis 12:10-16 or not? Why? What side of Sarah do you find in Genesis 16:1-6? What do you learn about being a Christian wife from Sarah's successes and failures?

3. Women living like Sarah must avoid a pitfall. What is it? (v. 6) List the reasons for fear Sarah had in Genesis 12:1, 4-5. Describe a situation where your anxiety has caused friction at home.

   For such a situation as this, write instructions to yourself based on James 5:13a and Proverbs 3:5-6.

Day 5: The groom and other kin Read 1 Peter 3:7.

1. Describe the perfect Christian husband. Do you think he exists? Is verse 7 written to Christian husbands or all husbands? (see 1:2)

2. Read verse 7 along with Ephesians 5:25 and in your own words tell how God describes a Christian husband. What positive connotation regarding the marital relationship does the word "partner" imply? What positive connotation does the fact that husbands and wives are heirs together imply?

A husband is to cherish his wife, but many women don't experience being cherished. To what promises can they cling? See Deuteronomy 33:27a and Isaiah 46:4.

All family members have a responsibility to make relationships work. Name the responsibility of:
❧ The child (Ex. 20:12; Eph. 6:1-3)

❧ Other family members (Rom. 15:2; Eph. 4:2-3)

Review this lesson and decide how you can enable your husband, child, or other family member to enjoy family life more.

Reflections Along The Way

If a gentle and quiet spirit were something I could purchase in a spiritual apparel shop, I'd be there when the doors opened. If it were a high-ticket item, I'd cut out anything not necessary to keep me alive in order to buy it.

Those weren't my exact thoughts during the years my inner woman was anything but tranquil, but they are a reasonable facsimile. Did I want to be a serene wife and mother—the kind Peter described as having spiritual beauty? Of course. In my mind's eye, I saw an idealized Marion whose ever-placid spirit was often admired by kin. In reality, quietness and gentility didn't come, though I prayed and studied and memorized and taught and bowed and begged.

Making matters worse were the sermons I heard and books I read, telling me peace came with surrender to Jesus. But I had surrendered—time and time again!

I felt like a Christian klutz—a woman who could do only three push-ups caught in a room full of exercise buffs. Did I have a case of spiritual retardation?

I especially remember one lunchtime: I was parked by a rural stream, eating my sandwich and reading a booklet by A.B. Simpson entitled *Himself*, in which he stated that all we need to live the sought-after life is Jesus Himself.

I eased back into the car seat and fantasized. *Children may scream and wail. The phone may jangle incessantly. Chicken pox may come and go, but none of these things will move me.*

Looking back I smile at the memory. How badly I wanted the Christian life to be a fairy tale with Jesus, my Prince, riding in and silencing my inner roaring!

During those years, I told no one my feelings, so I supposed I was the only one who felt that way. Since then, I have heard the experiences of others, like a single woman I know. "With my schedule? I'm anything but quiet. Every moment is taken up with something. I get up before sunrise, get ready for work, drop my daughter off at the sitter's, work all day, pick up my daughter, make the commute home. Then I begin a second day's work.

"On weekends, there are home repairs, housework, and a million errands. On Sunday there's church. On top of it all is the nagging guilt that I can't find time to play with my daughter the way I'd like. My mind is always going in six directions. I'm afraid I'm demonstrating frenzy to my daughter, not peace!"

An older woman in poor health remembered when she could face everyday tumult and remain calm. "But not now. I feel the signs of old age and it scares me. I worry about what the future holds for me. I so want to display Jesus' qualities before my family, but I don't think I'm doing a good job of it. That only makes me feel worse."

Failing to find the answer, women for whom the way to inner beauty is a distant dream often wear a skin-deep facade of tranquility. Secretly, they wonder what kernel of truth, what spirit-soaring experience they missed.

We do know that all we need is Jesus only. But we're too busy to do more about it than commiserate with ourselves because we're helping with a school fund-raiser, or trying to decide what to do about an elderly mother who lives alone and is failing.

The time comes when we must act on our dilemma. Either we can't stand the way we are, or our mate can't stand the way we are, or we can't get away with blaming others any longer. When that time came for me, I learned principles I've never forgotten.

Becoming beautiful is a process. We aren't living in a Disney film in which toads turn into princes. We're humans and must learn everything from the moment we're born. "Learn of Me," Jesus said, and not without reason.

Count on Jesus. His nature, reborn in us, provides us with the potential for natural beauty. Besides that, God has promised to recreate us in His image.

It requires hard work. To become spiritual beauties, we must cooperate with God by making a series of choices every day to deny our unregenerate tendencies and live in the power of the Holy Spirit.

Beauties follow regimens. Top models must eat carefully, exercise, and get plenty of sleep. Spiritual beauty also must be nurtured and nourished by reflecting on the Word of God and obeying it.

Relax and keep counting on God. Several times a day, take deep breaths and practice some form of relaxation. Focus on the fact that God Himself is in you, sharing your life. Think continuously about the implications of His presence as you work.

Know your personality. For some, quietness and gentility comes easily; others who are intense (like I am) become keyed up. Learn the little tricks it takes to be your best self.

Prioritize daily. Pare down. Determine to let go of work that you honestly can't do; live with the frustration until it dissipates (which it will). Don't expect more of yourself than God does. Keep in mind your primary goal: to become more beautiful spiritually.

Confide. Not just in anyone, but someone mature and insightful. You don't know such a person? Ask God to bring someone to you.

Expect ugly moments. No one is always dazzling. Even physical beauties develop ugly red pimples on their noses. Don't put yourself down. Find out what went wrong and learn from it.

Peace on the inside; chaos on the outside. We do become agitated, but if we keep fixing our inward focus on the presence of Jesus here and now, our spirits will grow serene again.

The very experiences from which we beg release are the ones God will use to beautify our inner woman. Look for His leading, grungy day after grungy day, and praise Him. As you do so, the beautifying process will be taking place.

No, you won't gasp in astonishment as you look in the mirror, but you'll sense a softening. And what's even better—your family will too.

DAY BY DAY WITH GOD

Day 1: Don't put this off Into which category do you fall? Very submissive but feeling used? Alternately submissive and independent? Not a submissive bone in your body? Decide what's keeping you from being balanced in the area of submission and one thing you can do to begin a change.

Day 2: Take inventory Are you dressing to impress people? If so, whom? Do you need to do something differently?

Day 3: Verse for women on the move Memorize 1 Peter 3:4 from the *Holy Bible, New International Version*: "[Your beauty] should be that of your inner self, the unfading beauty of a gentle and quiet spirit, which is of great worth in God's sight."

Day 4: Think about Sarah In order to be like her, you should "not give way to fear." What does that mean? What are you most afraid of right now? How can you deal with it? If you need to talk this over with someone who can help you work through it, do so.

Day 5: What does this bring to mind? Of the women of the first century, Warren Wiersbe says: "Christian wives were experiencing a whole new situation and needed guidance" (Wiersbe, *Bible Exposition Commentary*, Vol. 2, p. 410). How does that apply today, especially to family life? To you in particular?

BETWEEN FATHER AND DAUGHTER
Daily Prayer Suggestions

Day 1: "A good way to start being more submissive to a difficult family member is to show them respect. What I need to remember is that he or she is made in Your image — that's reason enough to show respect. You know the person I have in mind now."
    Pray also
   ❧ About particular problems you have with submission;
   ❧ To be able to let go of resentments that hinder you from submitting.

Day 2: "Some days I don't feel beautiful because I struggle with an ugly thought or I'm churned up inside. But You see right into me."
Pray also
 ❦ Committing yourself to spend a balanced proportion of time on your inside beauty and your physical appearance;
 ❦ To find someone who wants to grow in the same ways you do, so you can encourage one another.

Day 3: "You didn't expect the biblical women You used as examples to be perfect, Lord. I'm sure glad that You didn't want them on a pedestal. They were ordinary women, like me, and that helps me relate to them."
Pray also
 ❦ About any unhealthy tendency toward perfection you may have;
 ❦ For courage to live in communion with other women, not in isolation from them.

Day 4: "It wasn't easy for Sarah to uproot her life and follow Abraham when he didn't know where he was going. She must have had some anxiety. How I relate. I surrender to You the anxiety I have about the future."
Pray also
 ❦ For women missionaries you know who have to deal with frightening situations;
 ❦ Paraphrasing favorite passages about conquering fear.

Day 5: "So many marriages are in pain because husbands aren't living biblically. Work through every Christian ministry to reach them, Father."
Pray also
 ❦ For the spiritual growth of your husband or the husband of someone close to you;
 ❦ That ministries to families in your church will bear fruit.

6

WHEN IT'S HARD TO BE FAITHFUL
1 Peter 3:8-22

❦

YOUR FATHER WRITES

Day 1: Six ways to make life count Read 1 Peter 3:8-22; review verses 8-12.

1. If you could change how you handle a difficult person, what would you do differently? What differences could it make in your relationship?

Peter addresses several groups of Christians in 2:13–3:7. To whom is he speaking in 3:8? Discuss the instructions in verse 8 which would help in a difficult relationship.

A. *Live in harmony.* How is it possible for different Christians to do so? See Ephesians 4:3-6. How does this apply to your difficult relationship above?

B. *Be sympathetic . . . be compassionate.* The phrase "be compassionate" comes from a Greek word that means "fellow-feeling" (Wuest, *Word Studies in the Greek New Testament*, Vol. II, p. 85). What most often prevents you from having this attitude? How does this apply to your difficult relationship above?

C. *Love as brothers.* Peter means the human affection family members normally have toward one another. What first comes to mind when you think about this? How does it apply to your difficult relationship above? What are your conclusions about Peter's instructions?

2. A fourth instruction is given in verse 9. After reflecting on Matthew 5:38-48 and Romans 12:17-21, summarize verse 9 in a sentence which would be suitable for calligraphy. How does it apply to your difficult relationship?

3. Verses 10-12 are a reference to Psalm 34:12-16. The original language in 1 Peter 3:10 infers that we must chose to love life and that we must continue to do so. That's Paul's sixth instruction. What three suggestions for loving life does Psalm 34:13-14 give? What assurances? (vv. 15-16)

Day 2: Speaking up about Christ Read 3:13-15.

1. Imagine that you meet with an opportunity to witness to an acquaintance about Christ. How do you feel? Why?

In *The Amplified Bible*, verse 13 asks: "Now who is there to hurt you if you are zealous followers of that which is good?" How would you describe a "zealous follower of that which is good"? In other words, what are the qualities of such a woman?

What ordinarily happens if you do good? But Peter says that isn't always the case. What may happen instead? (v. 14a) Even if that happens, you are blessed. Which dictionary definition of the word *bless* most nearly expresses the meaning here?

2. Consult a second translation for verse 14b and write the essence of it in your own words. Note:
- ❦ Whom you are not to fear (Prov. 29:25);
- ❦ Whom you are to fear (Isa. 8:13);
- ❦ How Peter describes that kind of fear (1 Peter 1:17).

3. Read 3:15 in more than one translation. In order to witness, you are to sanctify or set apart Christ as Lord or Master. How will that help you be a witness?

Find words or phrases in 3:15b that answer these questions: What is our responsibility regarding witnessing? On what occasions are we to witness? What else do we learn from Isaiah 62:6? What's to be the focus on our message? How should we witness? What can we count on? (Acts 1:8)

Day 3: The value of a clear conscience Read 1 Peter 3:16-17.
1. Come up with a personal definition of conscience after consulting the dictionary. Think of a time when your conscience persistently condemned you for something. What effect did that have on your spiritual productivity?

   In order to be a witness, what kind of conscience must we maintain? What importance did Paul give to having a clear conscience? (See Acts 23:1; Acts 24:16; 1 Timothy 1:18-19.)

2. Do you think that you can always trust your conscience to tell you what's right and wrong? Read Romans 14:2 and 1 Corinthians 8:4, 7 and tell how one's conscience is affected by what one has been taught.

   Under what circumstances do you think a person's conscience would allow him or her to do evil? What do you need to do to develop a more trustworthy conscience? (Rom. 12:2; Col. 3:9-10)

3. What other reason is given in 1 Peter 3:16 for maintaining a clear conscience? How do we accomplish that? See Proverbs 28:13, Hebrews 9:14; 10:22.

Day 4: Knowing Noah Read 1 Peter 3:18-21a.

1. You want to be a faithful witness but are inconsistent. How can the following statements in verse 18 motivate you?
    - ❦ Christ died for my sins
    - ❦ Once for all
    - ❦ The righteous for the unrighteous
    - ❦ To bring me to God

    What two contrasting factors about Christ's death are described in verse 18? Which factor do you want most to remember?

2. Scholars differ as to the identity of the spirits in prison (v. 19), though many believe them to be disobedient angels from Noah's time. Noah is an outstanding example of one who was faithful under very difficult circumstances. Write summaries which emphasize:
    - ❦ The painful circumstances under which he built the ark;
    - ❦ The qualities that made him stand out (Gen. 6:9, 11-13, 22; 7:5). Based on this profile, what will you tell Noah when you meet him in heaven?

3. In what ways is the world you live in like the world of Noah's day? Especially consider the entertainment industry, politics, crime, and family life. Imagine you are called to be a witness in your town the way Noah was in his. After reading Matthew 24:37-41; 1 Corinthians 15:3-4; and 1 John 5:11-12, decide what you would say.

    For Noah, the ark was an ideal conversation starter about spiritual matters. What are some conversation starters you might use in three places where you spend time with non-Christians?

Day 5: Alive in Christ Read 1 Peter 3:21b-22.

1. Think of an object you own or wear which represents a loving relationship with someone. What is it and what does it symbolize?

What do each of the following symbols represent?

Symbol	What it represents
Sacrificial animals (John 1:29)	
Cross (Col. 1:19-20)	
Empty tomb (Luke 24:6a; John 11:24)	
Lord's Supper (Luke 22:19-20)	
Water baptism (Rom. 6:4)	

2. Describe Jesus' position and ministry from 3:22 *and* Ephesians 1:19-20; Philippians 2:9; Hebrews 7:24-25; and Revelation 5:12.

How is eternal life you possess described in John 17:3?

How do these possessions motivate you to respond to such things as bills that are due? Illnesses? Disappointments?

3. It's 5:30 P.M. and you're frazzled after a tough day. But you still have a lot of chores to complete. Write a personal translation of 1 Corinthians 15:58 which will energize you and pull you through.

Consult this week's schedule and decide which phrases in that verse you should remember in each key situation.

REFLECTIONS ALONG THE WAY

A long, bony finger waggles in your face and an accusing voice rasps: "How many souls have you won to Christ? How many?"

Your mouth seems to have forgotten how to form words. You moan garbled gibberish and awaken from your dream with the sounds still in your head. You feel as though you'd been through a shredder.

Why the nightmare? Was it the piece of cheesecake I ate before going to bed?

Probably not, you decide. More likely, it was the speaker at church yesterday who leaned over the pulpit and stuck his finger squarely on one of your most sensitive spots. The dream was your subconscious interpretation of his questions. "Are you winning souls for the kingdom? How many people will be in heaven because you led them to Christ?"

Many of us would have fingers left over if we were to count the people we've personally led to faith in Christ. I've certainly been made to sweat when other Christians confronted me with words about soul-winning.

Two incidents stand out. In the first, I was presented with a specific way to confront and lead someone to the Lord, but the idea sounded too aggressive to me. I was left wondering if I was a second-rate Christian if I weren't constantly witnessing to specific individuals about my faith, presenting the plan of salvation, and asking for a decision.

In the second incident, a new acquaintance spoke heatedly to me. "Committed Christians should be willing to go door-to-door in an attempt to lead people to Christ."

The compartment in my head labeled "soul-winning" definitely needed to be cleaned out and its contents reexamined. I needed to decide (1) what my biblical responsibility was when it came to sharing my faith; (2) what kept me from doing a better job; (3) what ways I could improve.

Jesus stated my biblical responsibility succinctly. "But you will receive power when the Holy Spirit comes on you; and you will *be My witnesses* in Jerusalem, and in all Judea and Samaria, and to the ends of the earth" (Acts 1:8, italics mine).

Like most of the women I know, I've been confused about exactly what a witness is and does. So I accumulated information and arranged it to form a whole.

John White explains that a witness is like a signpost. "It matters little whether the signpost is pretty or ugly, old or new. . . . The essential features are that it must point in the right direction and be clear about what it is pointing to. . . . Your witness will not focus on you but on the Christ you experience" (*The Fight*, Downers Grove, Ill.: InterVarsity Press, 1976, pp. 61–62).

We confuse witnessing with soul-winning, says Joseph Aldrich. "As long as a man simply tells another ABOUT Jesus, he is a witness. But the moment he tries to get that person to DO SOMETHING with Christ, he shifts over to the role of the soul winner" (Joseph C. Aldrich, *Life-style Evangelism*, Portland, Ore.: Multnomah Press, 1981, p. 19, quoting C.S. Lovett, *Witnessing Made Easy*).

My son John, in his parable "The Witness," put it all together. In his story, the main character is asked by a police officer if he'd testify about an accident he witnessed.

"I couldn't witness. I freeze up." The policeman is not impressed.

Finally, the main character understands. "Huh? I'm an *expert* on what happened? Just because I was the only one who *saw* it? . . . You say I already *am* a witness?" (John Duckworth, *Joan 'n' the Whale*, Old Tappan, N.J.: Fleming H. Revell Co., 1987, pp. 134–35)

So, a witness is to tell how she came to know Jesus and the place He's had in her life since. She's the only one who can tell that because she's the only human who's been a witness to that particular relationship.

She does need to be able to tell what Jesus saved her *from* and *for* and *how* He did it. Since she may even have an opportunity to lead the individual to Christ, she needs to know how.

But I have so few opportunities. I see the same people at work and in the neighborhood.

The Holy Spirit reminded me that in seeing the people in my world, I haven't necessarily seen them at all—not as people who have inside aches and unanswered questions. Nor have I consistently prayed for Him to initiate new opportunities to witness.

I know that I must follow Paula D'Arcy's advice: "Walk outside your house, trailer or apartment. Look in through a window. Now you see where God has sent you" (*Where the Wind Begins*, Wheaton, Ill.: Harold Shaw, 1984, p. 37).

It's because we *do* see the same people over and over that we have an advantage. Through those contacts, we can become friends, and out of that friendship, tell who Jesus is to us. The Holy Spirit will attune us to the loneliness of a neighbor; to the vulnerable quality beneath the chatter of the lady who cuts our hair.

Should we feel guilty if all we've done is tell a tiny fragment of the truth?

Not unless God gave a clear opportunity to tell more but we turned away out of fear that the other party would slam an invisible door shut in our face and we'd lose a friend. Still, we do often feel bound by our society's unwritten rule not to discuss religion. Besides, many of us just naturally want to avoid anything that smacks of confrontation.

What can we do about that? How can we become more facile witnesses?

There's no secret to it. We start where we are, praying for opportunities we can handle in the power of the Holy Spirit. At the same time, we let God refine our personalities so we won't be restricted by distortions in them.

We can rehearse ordinary situations in our minds; role play them in our women's groups; talk at home and among Christian friends about what God is doing for us; stand up in church despite our shaking knees and share again.

Every word spoken about Christ, no matter how seemingly insignificant, leaves us feeling a little surer—*We can do it.*

Since my visit to Oregon Caves, I've never underestimated the value that the tiniest flicker of light can have. It was in "The Ghost Room" that our guide turned out the lights, and we found ourselves in absolute darkness—not a tiny glimmer anywhere. I literally couldn't see my hand in front of my face.

Then the guide lit a match. For the seconds that it glowed, we could make out shapes and colors that had been completely obscured moments before. Now, years later, the scene it illuminated is still fixed in my mind.

That's the kind of light God is calling us to be on the daily bus ride, in sewing class, or in our neighborhoods. *You want me to be a match, Lord? I think I can manage that.*

DAY BY DAY WITH GOD

Day 1: Notice today the ways God has enabled you to "have a good day" and jot them down. Take time to tell someone about them. Complete these sentences: "I need to cultivate enthusiasm for life because . . . " and "I will cultivate enthusiasm for life even though . . . "

Day 2: Verse for a woman on the move As you memorize 1 Peter 3:15, decide (1) how you need to set aside Christ as Lord; (2) how you need to be prepared; and (3) what steps to begin taking.

Day 3: While you have free time today, think before God about the state of your conscience. Does something trouble you? Do you feel inwardly guilty? Do you ignore what it tells you? Do you need help in this area? Ask God for wisdom. Write and do what He shows you. Ask someone to check periodically on your progress.

Day 4: Think about this while you are in transit or waiting in line: "We find it difficult to witness because we have not learned how to be open" (John White, *The Fight*, p. 67). How true is that of you? What are you hiding, and why?

Day 5: Before bedtime choose one object as a symbol of Christ's resurrection (a plant or a picture, for example) and place it where you spend most of your time. Write here what you want the object to remind you of so that you'll be more consistently faithful—even when it's hard.

BETWEEN FATHER AND DAUGHTER
Daily Prayer Suggestions

Day 1: "I want to take the initiative to be loving and promote harmony in relationships where it's not so great. To do that, I need to get my focus off myself. People and problems with which I need special help are . . . "
Pray also
- For His Holy Spirit to guard your tongue and use it to glorify Himself;
- Giving thanks for all that God has provided to make your day good.

Day 2: "My life touches so many people who need to hear about You. I could be more vocal, I know. Things that keep me from doing that include . . . "
Pray also
- For insight into ways to be better prepared to articulate your faith;
- That God will lead you to the people who especially need to hear from you right now about Him.

Day 3: "Thank You for the gift of conscience. Show me how to make scriptural principles part of my thinking so that my sense of right and wrong will be more trustworthy. One area where I'm uncertain is ... "

Pray also

❦ To realize where you may be ignoring what's right;

❦ To be a better life witness in an area where you are now weak.

Day 4: "I confess the times when it's hardest to be faithful to You. One way I need help to change is ... "

Pray also

❦ For opportunities to start a conversation about spiritual matters;

❦ That you will keep in mind that fear is no reason to be unfaithful.

Day 5: "It's easy to take Christianity for granted. I think about the cross. The empty tomb. The meaning of Communion. My baptism."

Pray also

❦ Rejoicing to God for what these mean;

❦ Reflecting on the fact that, if you know Christ, you're a member of His everlasting kingdom *now*.

7

CHRISTLIKENESS IN SUFFERING
1 Peter 4:1-19

❧

YOUR FATHER WRITES

Day 1: When life hurts Read 1 Peter 4:1-19; review verses 1-6.
1. Draw a map indicating the places you go on an average day. List the unsaved people you encounter along the way who have in any way treated you badly because you're a Christian. In what ways have they done so?

How many times is the word "suffer" in all its forms used in this chapter? What conclusions do you draw? What kind of suffering is primarily referred to here? See 3:14a, 17.

A word related to "suffering" is "persecution." How does the dictionary define it? What definition does 1 Peter 4:16 give? Who do Ephesians 6:11-12 and Job 1:7-8 say is behind human suffering?

2. Imagine you are one of Jesus' disciples describing how He was persecuted on an average day, as recorded in John 8:48-59. What would you say? How did Jesus conduct Himself during His worst time of suffering? (1 Peter 2:23; Heb. 12:2-3)

What kinds of persecution have you experienced? If you've never experienced any, why do you think that is the case?

3. What do you possess in Christ that the people in question 1 do not? How does that shape your attitudes toward these people?

Day 2: Keeping perspective Read 1 Peter 4:7-9.
1. How do you organize your work? By making lists? Other ways? Write down as many projects as you can think of that you'd like to get done in the next three months.

What principle in 1 Peter 4:7 should you remember when you plan? Does it affect the way you view persecutors? How?

2. One important way to make our days count in these end times is to pray (v. 7). In order to pray, we must do two things:
   A. *Be clear minded.* What keeps you from concentrating during your daily prayer time? Write a reminder to use when you begin praying, based on Psalm 116:7.

   B. *Be self-controlled.* In what ways has lack of self-control interfered with your praying? According to these verses, what things should you pray for so you'll be most effective?

Scripture	Request
Matthew 26:41	
Ephesians 1:17-18	
Ephesians 3:14-19	
Philippians 1:9-11	
Colossians 1:9-12	

Which request will you start with?

In addition to praying, another way to make our days count in these end times is to love unselfishly and sacrificially. Where do we obtain that love? (Rom. 5:5)

3. Love leads to generous hospitality. What was there about first-century life that made hospitality essential? What kind of hospitality is important now?

Take stock of what you have available — time, lodging, or food, for example — and brainstorm new ways you can offer it. How will doing so bond you to those to whom you offer your time, lodging, or food?

Day 3: Using your gifts to minister Read 1 Peter 4:10-11.
1. Name some household gifts you've been given which benefit your whole family. What comparison can you make to the use of spiritual gifts? (1 Cor. 12:4-7)

First Peter 4:10-11 divides spiritual gifts into what two general groups? What gifts has God shown you that you have?

2. Which of the household gifts that you've received have you used most? What have been the results? What principle in Matthew 10:8 determines how you are to use your spiritual gifts?

Why do you suppose the Holy Spirit includes instructions on the use of your spiritual gifts in a section on suffering? Read 1 Thessalonians 5:11 and decide what you can do for others by using your particular gifts. How can that help you during persecution?

3. Reflect on the following thoughts from this passage and their ability to help alleviate suffering.
   ❦ My spiritual gifts are a result of God's grace.
   ❦ I can count on God to provide me strength to use my gifts.

Day 4: When the heat is on Read 1 Peter 4:12-13.
1. At lunch with friends, the discussion turns to Rhonda, a dedicated Christian who has terminal cancer. How might different people explain why this has happened?

In the beginning of verse 12 is what God calls you. Read it in more than one translation and decide how it influences your view of suffering.

Review the definition of "trial" from chapter 1. If you want to amplify it here, do so.

2. Suppose you are debating with someone who insists God wouldn't allow adversity to happen to a Christian who has real faith. Study verses 12-13 and James 1:2-3, 12 and formulate your reply.

Besides persecution, what other experiences are classified as trials? A trial is described as "painful" or "fiery" (KJV) — a word that literally means "a burning." In Psalm 66:10 and 1 Peter 1:6-7, what related truth do you find about why God allows such trials?

3. In order to increase understanding, consult several translations for the following reasons that we can rejoice in our suffering.
   ❦ Matthew 5:11-12

   ❦ Romans 5:3-4

   ❦ Romans 8:17

☙ 1 Peter 4:13

Day 5: What's in a name? Read 1 Peter 4:14-19.

1. In what different ways do people you know use the word "Christian"? Look in the dictionary for others.

In the Roman Empire, Caesar was worshiped as a god. Believers who worshiped Jesus Christ and not Caesar came to be called "Christians." What information about the term do you learn from the three places in the New Testament where that word is used?

☙ Acts 11:26

☙ Acts 26:28

☙ 1 Peter 4:16

If you lived in the first century, how would you explain to a woman acquaintance what a Christian was? Suppose she asks you, "How does one become a Christian?" What would you answer, keeping in mind that she worships Caesar?

2. What kind of suffering might you undergo in each of the following circumstances?

☙ You buy a store in which you refuse to stock beer and cigarettes.

☙ You go to the school board to object because evolution is being taught as fact.

☙ The family in which you were raised says that only ignorant people believe the Bible is God's revelation.

What does verse 14 say you should realize when you are persecuted? Can persecution be an indication that you are living for the Lord? Why or why not?

3. Examine verse 19, which sums up the chapter. Reflect also on related passages listed below with each phrase of verse 19. Write your thoughts.

   ❦ "Those who suffer according to God's will" — 1 Peter 4:15

   ❦ "Should commit themselves to their faithful Creator" — 2 Timothy 1:12

   ❦ "And continue to do good" — Galatians 6:9

You are designing a T-shirt with a motto that includes the word "Christian." What would it say?

Reflections Along The Way

Life on earth ended at age 40 for Carla, a wife and mother, following a long battle with cancer. She'd written letters to me and certain other friends shortly before she passed on and asked that they be mailed to us afterward. Receiving Carla's letter was one of the most stunning experiences of my life. I was prepared for her to die. What I was not prepared for, though, was for her to thank me in a letter a week after she died for helping her through the hard times.

Carla was one of the most earnest Christians I knew. She longed to be Christlike, and pored over the Scriptures persistently for new insights. Still, Carla suffered and died.

That settled it for me. The Christian life is no fairy tale, and God is not a heavenly Superman who swoops down and plucks good little followers safely out of every perilous circumstance.

"If there is anything real in life, it is pain" (Susan Perlman. *Issues*, Vol. 6.6, San Francisco: Jews for Jesus, p. 1). Deep inside, most of us know that. Still, we recoil in horror when pain — physical, mental, or emotional — happens to us.

Why does suffering come as such a slashing surprise? For one thing, Americans have been plagued with the unbiblical philosophy that "good Christians live happily ever after." When I hear the TV happiness hawkers drool that we can "believe and grow rich and healthy," I want to scream back at them, "You mean like Stephen, who was stoned to death? Like James, who was beheaded by Herod? Or Paul, who was stoned, beaten, and imprisoned?"

Besides, when it's our own hands and feet that are in the stocks or our own heads in the noose, we respond from an experiential, not intellectual, level. Then our human nature cries out to stop the pain, and our conscience insists that it's all our fault. Truth is obscured by feeling. Whether through cancer or desertion or persecution, it's as though someone's lashed us to the bottom side of life and the only direction we can see is down.

Few things in life are as important as planning for the times when we'll suffer or for the times when one of the Carla's in our lives will. Peter implies in 1 Peter 4:1 that, in order to survive with our faith intact, we need the heavy, defensive armor of biblical certainties.

❦ *Faith for the fire comes from God.* When the heat is on, dialogue with God from the outset with your Bible open. To gain a solid spiritual footing, do so for as long as it takes and as often as it takes. Reflect on who He is and what He reveals about Himself. Write important truths in your journal.

❦ *Faith is a spiritual quality and not an emotion.* When I had cancer, I experienced the emotion of fear. Before too long, I recognized that in my spirit I was simultaneously sensing tranquility and confidence. I saw again that we Christians live on two levels—human and spiritual—at the same time. As we focus on the presence and power of the Holy Spirit, peace and confidence and faith gradually become more predominant than the emotion of fear. In time we are more able to choose to live by what we know, not by what we feel.

❦ *God has people who will help us.* Carla's posthumous thank-you will always remind me that we should never go through trial alone. God has believers who will go through it with us, ministering through their gifts. There may not *seem* to be anyone, but there is. If we ask expectantly, God will show us who those persons are. We may have to let them know, though, that we need support.

❦ *Joy in trial grows out of what we know.* Christians aren't masochists who delight in pain. We can rejoice, not because suffering feels good, but because the Scriptures assure us that our trials have eternal purposes, such as preparing us to reign with Christ.

Every moment "the Lord our God [is with us] to help us and to fight our battles" (2 Chron. 32:8). We may *seem* to be alone fighting specters during never-ending nights, but that's because we're temporarily unaware of things as they really are.

Take, for example, the cub in the film *The Bear*. When suddenly confronted by a big cat, the cub roared as fiercely as he could. He swiped at the cat who, in turn, lunged and wounded the cub's muzzle. Again the cub roared—and suddenly the cat turned and fled. The camera panned back. There, behind the cub, was his ever-loyal friend—a 1,500-pound Kodiak bear, standing upright and roaring angrily at the fleeing enemy.

An imposing figure, to be sure. But nothing at all, compared to the One who is with us. "The Lord is my refuge . . . in whom I trust" (Ps. 91:2).

DAY BY DAY WITH GOD

Day 1: Listen to yourself Instead of talking naturally about God, are you censoring your conversation with non-Christians (deciding not to mention an answer to prayer, for example), so they won't think of you negatively? Do you wear two faces—one with Christians, one with non-Christians? How can you integrate your two selves? You may want to ask someone to pray consistently with you about this and encourage you to change.

Day 2: Every time you think of it today If people could see inside your head, would they see chaos or calmness? Find ways to turn your thoughts into prayers. Be especially sure to include your worries over difficult circumstances. As you do so, note changes you experience.

Day 3: Today wear something multicolored and reflect on the fact that God has created Christians with many-colored talents. Think of a couple of occasions when Christians have used their talents and helped you when you were undergoing trials.

Day 4: Verse for a woman on the move Memorize 1 Peter 4:13. Remember as you do so that you're not sinful if you express doubts and cry when your trials are painful. You can rejoice because of what you *know*, not how you *feel*.

Day 5: Take a walk and think of at least three reasons that you're thankful you're a Christian; then praise God. Or (if the weather is inclement), do the same as you relax and listen to music. Think about what your faith has meant to you during trials.

BETWEEN FATHER AND DAUGHTER
Daily Prayer Suggestions

Day 1: "It's hard not to be resentful when someone treats me cruelly. But Jesus, You took that pain in Your body, so I don't have to carry it around. The situation I need to entrust to You is . . . "
Pray also
❦ To be able to see with compassion those who've hurt you;
❦ To become aware of ways to minister to them.

Day 2: "Are there things in my life that are hindering my prayers' effectiveness? Nothing is more important than knowing that, so I'm asking You to search me now."
Pray also
❦ Using 1 Peter 4:7-9 as your guide;
❦ That God will lead you as you plan your schedule.

Day 3: "Am I using my spiritual gifts the way You want? Maybe I'm not even aware of an ability You want me to use. If so, show me."
Pray also
❦ That God will be glorified through the use of your gifts;
❦ That others you know will use their gifts for Him.

Day 4: "So many questions about suffering remain unanswered. That's OK, Father. I'm not asking for answers, but to learn a right attitude from your Spirit toward suffering. I think especially of . . . "
Pray also
❦ To see ways to comfort others who are suffering;
❦ Using Scripture in Day 4 as reasons to rejoice.

Day 5: "I think about what being a Christian means. That word is used in all kinds of ways. Some of the things it means to me are . . . "
Pray also
❦ To grow strong enough to suffer gladly because you're a Christian, if it is necessary;
❦ Resolving to do whatever it takes to grow in that way.

8

DISCIPLING AND BEING DISCIPLED
1 Peter 5:1-7

❦

YOUR FATHER WRITES

Day 1: Christian leaders Read 1 Peter 5:1-7; review verse 1.
1. Describe a time when your church helped you during a trying situation. Describe a time when the church failed to help you. Was it partly your fault? If so, why?

Who led the local church that Peter writes about in verse 1? What are they called in verse 2? How does Peter, who was a leader in the early church, describe himself in verse 1? What is the title of the leader(ship) of the church you attend?

2. Though you don't share Peter's position or experience, you are called to be a leader in your church. Read the qualities of a church leader in 1 Timothy 3:2-7. List the ones that are required of all Christians. What does that tell you about the level of spirituality God expects in His churches?

3. We should keep growing spiritually so we'll be more effective leaders. How does Peter tell us to do that in:
    ❦ 1 Peter 2:2
    ❦ 2 Peter 1:5a
    ❦ 2 Peter 3:18?

Name one way you need to grow spiritually in order to minister more effectively in your church.

4. While we Christians may not be able to solve one another's problems or alleviate trials, in what practical ways can we help?
    ❦ Luke 22:40
    ❦ 1 Corinthians 16:1-2a
    ❦ Galatians 6:2

Can you think of others?

Day 2: Following the leader Read 1 Peter 5:2-3.
1. What would you do to care for sheep? What are the similarities to ministering to Christians who need your help.

How can you tell which of the many people you encounter who are in pain are the ones God means you to shepherd? See James 1:5.

2. Related to caring for the sheep is another ministry which Christians are to perform — described as "mak[ing] disciples" in Matthew 28:19a. Who spoke those words? Write the dictionary definition of "disciple" that fits best.

As we disciple others, whom should we urge them to follow? (John 10:27; also see Col. 3:1-14) Summarize your conclusions about a discipler's responsibilities.

3. What is to be your motivation for ministry? (1 Peter 5:2) Speak from your experience: How does good motivation affect what you do and how you do it?

Mary, the mother of Jesus, is an example of a woman who could have let herself become self-important because of her position. Instead, what words and phrases in Luke 1:46-55 express her attitude?

Day 3: Learning from our leader Read 1 Peter 5:4.

1. Think of a time when you learned to do something by watching another person. What did you learn? What one thing stands out about that experience?

   One way we learn to minister to others is by observing Christ who, in 1 Peter 5:4, is described as the Chief Shepherd. What word does Christ use in John 10:11, 14 to amplify that description of Himself? How do verses 11 and 15 say He would prove that was true?

2. What additional information do you find in Isaiah 40:11 about the Chief Shepherd?

   Reflect on ways Jesus fulfilled His role as Shepherd. Put together some guidelines for ministering to others.
   - Luke 4:42-44
   - Luke 14:27
   - Luke 15:3-7
   - John 1:35-39

3. Recall and describe your feelings when you received an award or high compliment for an achievement.

   First-century Christians would compare the crown mentioned in 1 Peter 5:4 to one made of fresh leaves and presented at athletic games, or made of flowers for marriage feasts. To what honor in your life would you compare the crown? What promise of God in verse 4 makes this crown different from any we receive in this life?

   The people he has influenced, says Paul in 1 Thessalonians 2:19-20, are his real crown. Based on those verses, what would you like to tell people who have influenced you?

Day 4: Women teaching women Read 1 Peter 5:5a.
1. Approximately how old are you as a Christian? Would you categorize yourself spiritually as a baby, child, youth, young adult, middle-aged woman, or senior citizen?

God's instructions about older people in verse 5a are part of His larger teaching in this letter. (See 2:13, 18; 3:1.) How would you summarize that teaching?

2. Is spiritual maturity or physical maturity more important in being a discipler? What insight do you gain from 1 Timothy 4:12?

State three desirable characteristics in older women, as stated in Titus 2:3. According to verses 3-4, what general subjects should they teach younger women? What other subjects especially pertinent today do you think they should teach?

3. What kind of teaching might a woman young in years do if she has experienced things like abuse or a dysfunctional homelife? What kinds of things did you need to learn when you were a new Christian? What opportunities do you have to help other women learn these things that you may not have thought of before?

Day 5: When down is better Read 1 Peter 5b-7.
1. What is your gut reaction when someone points out a flaw of yours? Why?

Look up the definition of "humble." Especially note its origin, if given, and write it down. Reflect on Jesus' illustration of humility in John 13:5 and Philippians 2:8 and write your thoughts.

First-century slaves wore aprons under which they arranged their outer garments for better mobility. *The Amplified Bible* reflects that idea: "Clothe (apron) yourself, all of you, with humility—as the garb of a servant, so that its covering cannot possibly be stripped from you" (5:5). What attitudes are preventing you from a working relationship with humility? What places where you spend your time do you need it most, and why?

2. What experience in Matthew 26:69-75 humbled Peter? What ex-

perience humbled you most? What did you learn from it? How does God's attitude toward pride in 1 Peter 5:5b reinforce your determination to learn humility?

The New Testament teaches that we must go down in order to get up. Compare 1 Peter 5:6 with Philippians 2:5-11 and put that principle into your own words.

3. If a single small worry weighed one pound and a large one weighed ten pounds, how much do you estimate you carry around on a bad day?

Scripture tells you: "You can throw the whole weight of your anxieties upon Him, for you are His personal concern" (1 Peter 5:7, Phillips' *New Testament in Modern English*). Reflect on the word "throw." What illustration comes to mind? How does it relate here? What conclusions do you draw?

REFLECTIONS ALONG THE WAY

Acting as sheep-sitter for my son's ewe when he was a member of 4-H was one of my "above and beyond the call of mothering" chores. I was filling that role one afternoon when I heard the ewe bleating repeatedly. On investigation, I discovered that she'd gotten her head stuck in a small hole in the fence and couldn't figure how to get it out.

I pushed. She bleated. I twisted and turned and pushed some more. She stood firm—a bleating, woolly monolith. "All those uncomplimentary things they say about sheep are certainly true," I muttered.

Looking her straight in the eye, I let her have it: "You're stupid." As if to prove I was right, she stayed put. Then finally, she backed out of the hole.

I realized later that the ewe wasn't the only dumb one. My ignorance about shepherding put me in the same category. Years later, when I read accounts of those men and women and their flocks in Bible days, I marveled.

Sheep and shepherd developed a relationship. They bonded to him so completely that they recognized his voice and followed him out to pasture in the morning and back to the sheepfold at night.

Shepherds cared. The shepherds were attentive day after day, leading their charges to water and pasture, protecting against animals, birds of prey, and snakes. They knew when the sheep needed rest from the scorching sun and showed them where to find it.

Night after night as the flock passed under the caregiver's rod at the door of the sheepfold, he ran his hand over their bodies to check for wounds—perhaps from briars pressing against their flesh—and applied oil for healing when necessary. Then he lay down in the doorway so wild animals or sheep stealers couldn't snatch any of his flock away.

The toughness of the job didn't stop them. Every waking hour, the shepherd had to be alert. Working conditions were not good; food was limited; the weather was hot, dusty, and parching. Besides, the shepherds were missing family dinners and village celebrations.

The analogy was so obvious that it smacked me in the face. While most of us women are not undershepherds or pastors, we are called to extend care to people who need us. Often, they are limping, bruised, and wounded.

If ever a generation needed faithful shepherds, it is ours. Who has a better opportunity to fill that role than we do? We are office workers with desks next to mothers whose kids are in trouble. We are homemakers shopping alongside neighbors whose marriages are breaking up. We are committee members who notice fellow volunteers' long, distracted silences, their deep sighs, and distant stares.

We can ignore the signals they send for help, of course. After all, we're busy—booked up. Just as we're ready to hustle along, however, we sense Someone urging us to slow down and look more closely. The moment of truth: Will we listen and obey or brush God away and deny that it was Him at all?

Above all, to make our lives count while we're on the move, we must follow the Chief Shepherd. Only from Him can we know which among the hurting people in our workplace, community, and church are the ones He has for us. That means a commitment to live in the Spirit so we're able to hear His voice.

Theresa, a schoolteacher, listened. Her sheep were kids in her high school classroom. "So many of them need mothering. They'd stop by my desk after class to talk. They desperately needed me to care about them." And by becoming involved in their lives, she did.

Exactly what do we do for them besides listening, encouraging, and expressing God's love? Lambs outside God's flock may be ready to hear about our personal relationship with Him and how they can know Him themselves. Those whose wounds are deep will probably need a professional who can facilitate inner healing, and we can encourage them to contact one. Women who came to Christ but are floundering will need to know how to live as Christians. They may have very practical needs, such as learning how to live on a budget or finding medical help they can afford.

One thing I've learned is that God has pretty unorthodox ways to bring wounded sheep and me together, so I'd better be paying attention. I certainly wasn't doing that the morning Eva's car ran out of gas in front of my house. If my husband Jack hadn't called me away from the book I was writing, I wouldn't have chosen to meet her at all. *Got to finish this paragraph. Got to meet this deadline.* But Eva and I did become acquainted, and I learned she was a Christian looking for a women's fellowship to meet with—perhaps on her lunch hour.

I knew of none but suggested we two have lunch. Over sandwiches each week, we became acquainted and eventually, Eva showed me the painful places she kept carefully hidden from view. I understood, because I'd experienced and dealt with many of the things she was facing, so I was able to suggest ways to find healing.

If we begin to think that we're upper echelon because we're shepherding others, we need only remember: *We are both sheep and shepherds*—the divine paradox that binds us inextricably together.

DAY BY DAY WITH GOD

Day 1: Take a good look Are you so tied to your agenda in church affairs that you don't see or respond to people who need help? What are your priorities? Note what you can do to be more effective.

Day 2: Think today about the person who has done the most to disciple you. In what ways did he or she contribute to your growth? What can you learn from him or her about discipling others?

Day 3: Verse for a woman on the move Memorize 1 Peter 5:4.

Picture that event from what you know in the New Testament. Use the verse as motivation and encouragement when you need it most.

Day 4: Evaluate What practical, household, or relational skills could you teach other women? Or what spiritual disciplines, such as studying the Bible, molding a child's character, keeping a journal, or dealing with particular problems?

Day 5: Keep in mind To be discipled yourself, you need to be humble. To disciple others, you need to be humble as well. Jot down as many reasons as you can think of to explain why that's true. What is the Holy Spirit showing you here?

BETWEEN FATHER AND DAUGHTER
Daily Prayer Suggestions

Day 1: "I want to be closer to the women in my church—to see more of them as Christian sisters. Show me—are there things I can do to make that happen?"
Pray also
❧ For your church leaders;
❧ To see ways you yourself can be more effective.

Day 2: "Sensitize me to people in places where I spend my time who need my help. Remind me that the things I think I absolutely must get done are probably less important than helping a human soul."
Pray also
❧ To be led by the Spirit when God gives an opportunity to help someone;
❧ Asking Him to examine your motives for ministry.

Day 3: "How can we improve the discipling program in our church? Raise up leadership, Father. Encourage people who need help to let others know. Bring persons to them who have the needed skills."
Pray also
❧ Giving thanks for God shepherding you in particular ways;
❧ For hurting children you know who need to experience His care.

Day 4: "Forgive me for times when pride has kept me from asking for help when I've needed it. Do in me whatever is necessary so I won't let that happen in the future."

Pray also

❧ To be aware of ways you may now need help, and be open enough to ask for it;

❧ For new Christians you know who need to be discipled.

Day 5: "I've fallen into such a habit of internalizing my anxieties instead of giving them to You. And when I do pray about them, I don't really *cast* them on You in a once-for-all commitment. Lord, I'm going to try to do that right now."

Pray also

❧ That God will help you make this casting of cares a habit;

❧ Thanking God for this privilege.

9

STANDING FIRM
1 Peter 5:8-14

YOUR FATHER WRITES

Day 1: Warning: DANGER AHEAD! Read 1 Peter 5:8-14; review verse 8.

1. Under what conditions are you most easily tempted? Review the definition of *trial* in Study 1, Day 4. Look up *tempt* in the dictionary.

Read 1 Peter 5:8-9 again. Would you say then that defeating Satan is your job or God's job? A cooperative effort between the two of you? Why?

Two things you are to do are described in verse 8a.
   A. Be *sober*, or self-controlled. Consult your dictionary and other translations and write a definition that's clear to you.

   B. Be *alert*, or vigilant. Matthew 24:43; 26:40; and Acts 20:28-31 contain this same word (translated "watch" in the *King James Version*). After looking at these passages, write an expanded definition of being alert or watching. Note also how being self-controlled and alert relate to one another.

2. What names is Satan called in the following references? What personal warnings do you see in each?

	Name	Personal warning
Matthew 4:3		
Matthew 13:19		
2 Corinthians 4:4		
Ephesians 2:2		
Revelation 12:10		

What are Satan's followers called in 1 Timothy 4:1?

Summarize what to remember about Satan when the dishes are piled high, money is scarce, and you have a headache. Since these things are true, how could jokes about Satan be harmful?

3. What precautions would you take in a land where lions prowled? How do they apply to living in a world where Satan prowls?

Day 2: Stand firm Read 1 Peter 5:9.
1. Think of a childhood game where you tried to knock your opponent off balance, and vice versa. How did you keep from being moved? How do those tactics illustrate the principle in verse 9?

2. You need to begin the day prepared for Satan's interference. Write a series of statements based on Ephesians 6:10-18 to use as a personal checklist. Remember that each piece of armor corresponds to a kind of spiritual defense we can use. Consult a paraphrased translation, if you wish. Begin the checklist this way:
     ❦ (v. 10) "My strength to defeat Satan is in the Lord's power over him."
     ❦ (v. 13)

     ❦ (v. 14)

❦ (v. 15)

❦ (v. 16)

❦ (v. 17)

❦ (v. 18)

3. Should you be surprised that evil exists and Satan causes you pain? Write a reminder to yourself based on the truths in 5:9b and Romans 8:17-18.

Read and reflect on Hebrews 2:14. Who defeated Satan for you? How did he do it? What can we do every time Satan tempts us?

Day 3: Count on God Read 1 Peter 5:10.
1. Describe physical exercises you've done and the parts of your body they made stronger. Who will strengthen you spiritually, according to 1 Peter 5:10? Name one way He does it.

"The phrase 'the God of all grace' speaks of God as the source of all spiritual comfort and help for every occasion" (Wuest, *Word Studies in the Greek New Testament,* Vol. 2, p. 130). For what troublesome situations do you need comfort and help right now?

2. Look up the word "glory" in the dictionary. In what way has God given us "glory in Christ" (v. 10) now? In what way will He do so in the future?

The three specific qualities in which you'll grow after you've suffered awhile (v. 10) are . . . How do you think they will make you a better Christian?

3. Since you can count on suffering to be a regular part of your life, how can your attitude toward it influence others in a positive way? Before you answer, think how others' attitudes toward suffering have influenced you.

Why was Stephen able to face the ultimate suffering—death—and still express strong faith in God? (see Acts 7:55) How can we face our own hard times in the same way? (see Eph. 5:18b)

Day 4: Hallelujah! Read 1 Peter 5:11.

1. What have been your most memorable times of praising God? Did they take place when you felt good or when your spirits were low? Or both?

What does Hebrews 13:15 intimate about praising God when it's hard? Grade yourself on how strong a habit you've formed of praising God during the course of the day (circle one):

      A   B   C   D   F

2. Peter bursts forth with praise in verse 11. Reread 1:3-5 and list reasons to praise which Peter states there. What new thoughts come to you about God's ability to use suffering for your good? What new insight do you gain from Romans 8:28-29?

Sing a praise chorus as your response to God.

3. *The Amplified Bible* version of verse 11 reads: "To Him be the dominion—power, authority, rule—forever and ever. Amen—so be it." Read the references below and describe what they mean to you:

   ❦ The dominion of God (Ps. 103:19)

   ❦ The power of God (Matt. 19:26)

   ❦ The authority of God (Isa. 43:13)

   ❦ The rule of God (Ex. 15:18)

With those characteristics in mind, continue to praise God—this time in prayer. How does praise help defeat Satan?

Day 5: In closing Read 1 Peter 5:12-14.

1. Name two truths you would like your life to demonstrate. Verses

12-14 are a P.S., probably written in Peter's own handwriting, that state truths very important to him. What are they?

How does he describe Silas, also called Silvanus, to whom he may have dictated this letter? What do you learn about him from verse 12 and Acts 15:22-27, 30-34?

2. People in the early church demonstrated their love for one another with a holy kiss. How do you demonstrate love to sisters in the Lord? Why does doing so help Christians remain faithful to Him?

What loving actions—like speaking an encouraging word, giving a hug when appropriate, writing a note—do you need to practice? Which do you need to act on *now*?

Next, reflect on the final line of the letter. To whom is peace available? (v. 14b) What habit do you need to form in order to know peace? (Phil. 4:6-7) What promise is made?

If you had been present and heard Jesus speak about peace (see John 14:27), what would you have written in your journal afterward?

REFLECTIONS ALONG THE WAY

One of my favorite places to spend a sunny afternoon is the zoo. I always stop a good while near the entrance because that's where the lions are located.

It's a funny thing, though. I don't ever remember hearing the lions roar. Mostly they sleep peacefully. And why not? They have plenty of food and no enemies with whom to do battle. So they just lie there in the sun on their backs with their soft-looking bellies up. I look at them and think: *Nice kitties.*

Of course, I know better. Even in captivity, the lion is not a nice kitty. Zoo visitors who have gotten too close to lions' cages have learned that. Even in captivity, the big cat is still a predator. A lion is a lion is a lion.

That's true of his spiritual counterpart, Satan, too. But unconsciously, at least, we do seem to suppose that we're reasonably safe from him because we live in a civilized society, for one thing. *Surely Satan doesn't prowl and roar here*, we think.

After all, we aren't primitives who worship evil spirits or offer blood sacrifices to stone idols. We are wise, cultured, and erudite, and have Christian churches everywhere.

On the other hand, we see Satan in people who live separated from God. It's easy to see him in the faceless bad guys whose evil makes our stomachs turn. But we're the good guys. We tithe and pray and take our kids to Bible Club. We know Jesus Christ personally—and He's defeated Satan for us. So why shouldn't we feel secure?

That's a mistake. John White sets us straight when he says, "You personally are of no interest to him [Satan]. It is only as you relate to Christ that you assume significance in his eyes" (John White, *The Fight*, p. 78).

Since every daughter of God is related to Christ, Satan is unquestionably an enemy of each of them. Roaring, growling, or purring, he will attack. To think otherwise is to believe a myth.

There are other myths that we need to dispel if we're going to overcome him while we're tromping around the planet he rules.

Myth: Christ's victory over Satan means that we can sail through life.

Fact: Christ indeed did defeat Satan for us, but we must appropriate His victory every time we confront the evil one.

Myth: Saying a Bible verse will automatically deliver us from the power of the evil one.

Fact: What's necessary is to *choose to count on* a particular truth in spite of feelings of doubt or anxiety, and not merely to repeat passages like incantations.

Myth: Satan only tempts important Christians.

Fact: Every Christian is fair game because every Christian is important to God.

Several years ago when I found myself tripped up by the deceiver one more time, I began pouring over Scripture to see how, in practical terms, we could win over him. What I learned was that the first step is to recognize that we *will* be tempted, regardless of who we are or who we think we are.

How do we know? Perhaps because our sense of well-being is eroded. And while it may stem from a natural cause, like premenstrual syndrome or menopause, Satan will take advantage of any debilitating situation if we let him.

Resisting him means, for one thing, getting whatever help is available—whether for our hormones or our emotions. Resisting also means seeing temptation for what it is—part of living as a Christian in this world. Therefore, being tempted is not the sin, but yielding to it is.

When I am mentally, emotionally, or physically ragged, any temptation can seem overwhelming. At such times, I employ an emergency plan.

❦ *Kneel and pray.* Kneeling will remind you that you are a created being, wholly dependent on God. Or, if you can't kneel, prostrate before God in humility in your mind.

❦ *Tell God everything—all that you are thinking and feeling.* Take as much time as you need. Show Him all your feelings. Actually *feel* them before Him.

❦ *Worship.* Slowly focus on the presence of God—on a particular name of His—like Jehovah, for example. Talk or sing to Him about His greatness.

❦ *Meditate on Scripture.* Let God lead you to an appropriate passage. Allow Him to expose wrong attitudes. Confess and agree with Him about them. Continue to worship Him as Lord; focus on Him as a present helper.

❦ *Confront evil with truth.* Keep it centered in your mind that "the reason the Son of God appeared was to destroy the devil's work" (1 John 3:8). And He did. Tell God you're trusting Him to defeat the evil one. When doubt or despondency swells, return to the choice you've made to let Him fight for you. Do not allow yourself to be intimidated.

❦ *Believe in what you know—not in what you feel.* You may *feel* defeated—but because of Christ, you *are* victorious. Choose to believe that. Keep worshiping Him as Lord of all. Moment by moment, count on God to fill you with Himself (Eph. 3:19).

Most of all, be sure you know your lions. "Do not weep! See, the Lion of the tribe of Judah, the Root of David, has triumphed" (Rev. 5:5).

DAY BY DAY WITH GOD

Day 1: What do I think about this? "You will be tempted. The kinds of temptation may change: Candies for kids, sensuality for the young, riches for the middle aged and power for the aging" (John White, *The Fight*, p. 78). Are you described here? What is God showing you?

Day 2: Verse for a woman on the move As you memorize 1 Peter 5:8-9a, ask yourself which of your spiritual defensive weapons you need to make stronger. What is one practical way you can do that now? Note: It's dangerous to postpone this.

Day 3: When your mind is undistracted Think about the contemporary person whose attitude in suffering has been exemplary because of his or her strength, firmness, and steadfastness. What makes this person that way?

Day 4: Make a joyful noise Spend five minutes praising God in ways that use your mind, emotions, and spirit. What change did that make in you?

Day 5: Make time to rest in God On a scale of 1–10 (1 being the least), how peaceful are you? Is your peace a facade or does it go deep inside? Set aside five minutes to experience peace by relaxing your whole body as you sit in God's presence. Choose one of the names of Christ on which to focus, such as Lamb or Lord. Write your thoughts.

BETWEEN FATHER AND DAUGHTER
Daily Prayer Suggestions

Day 1: "I go my way, ignoring Satan for the most part, Lord. It's true that I don't want to be preoccupied with him, but I don't want to be deceived by him either. Is this happening? Please give me insight."
Pray also
- ❦ To become aware of specific ways Satan tempts you — through TV, video, or reading material, for example;
- ❦ To become aware of attitudes that give him a foothold, such as, resentments you may be harboring against someone.

Day 2: "I don't resist certain kinds of evil very well. I get tired and want to quit. I want to compromise, though I know that's wrong."
  Pray also
  ❦ To better understand the different weapons God has given to fight Satan and how you can better use them;
  ❦ To learn to apply Christ's victory over Satan.

Day 3: "Please use whatever trials You allow to mature me. Train me to stand firm. One trial that comes to mind is . . . "
  Pray also
  ❦ To be able to count on God's spiritual comfort and help when you're most vulnerable;
  ❦ For others you know who are suffering now to do so as well.

Day 4: "All praise to You, Father. The reasons are endless. There's the amazing fact that You love me and wanted me to be Your own daughter. And You became a man and defeated Satan so that could happen. Other reasons I think of to praise You are . . . "
  Pray also
  ❦ To be able to praise during hard times;
  ❦ Thank God that He who has complete dominion, power, authority, kingship, and rule has become your Savior.

Day 5: "How I want to be faithful! That my life will honestly count for You is my prayer. Show me little ways that can happen today and every day. Stop me short when I pull away from You."
  Pray also
  ❦ To be aware daily of ways to show and carry out God's love;
  ❦ For insight about faithfulness from the Scriptures.

INTRODUCTION

The women in your Bible study group are probably as diverse as threads in a tapestry. Yet singles, harried mothers, professional women, and homemakers alike have one thing in common: *they want their lives to count.*

As a group leader, you can help them reach that goal by making use of the women's personal similarities and differences. Because we women share similar needs and feelings despite age or status, we are in a position to minister to one another. But because we are different, we can awaken others to see life from a fresh perspective. By encouraging balanced group discussion and drawing out quiet members, you can do this.

Note: In the leader's guide, the questions you will take the group through (which are designated Day 1, for example) are taken from *Your Father Writes*, unless otherwise indicated.

❦ Guide discussion so members will relate biblical principles to real-life situations. Keep in mind issues relevant and common to the group: too much work and too little time or energy; feeling overburdened; experiencing a sense of futilty over doing meaningless work; dealing with a sense of isolation in an uncaring, un-Christian society. Be willing to share yourself and your own experiences. By example, encourage others to do the same without pressuring them.

❦ Be sure everyone is keeping up. You may have women in your group who are not believers or who are unfamiliar with the Bible. Give them time and help—assign them partners. Take advantage of sessions where the subject of the new birth comes up by briefly presenting the Gospel. Remember to follow up.

❦ Vary the way Scripture is read—for example, sometimes using volunteers, with each reading a verse; or reading in chorus.

❦ Pray as a group to foster greater bondedness among members. Use ideas in *Between Father and Daughter* as a springboard but take other requests too. Bring variety to the prayer time: break into small groups and assign one day's prayer guides to a group; or form a circle and pray sentence prayers; or use conversational paryer. Provide the option for those who wish to pray silently.

Tips for Leaders
Preparation

❦ Pray for the Holy Spirit's guidance as you prepare, so you will be equipped to lead the lesson and make it applicable. Pray for your participants personally; ask God to help them as they work through the study prior to the session; and pray for the meeting's impact.

❦ Gather and/or prepare any materials you or the group will need.

❦ Read through the entire lesson and related Scriptures. Answer the questions for yourself.

The Meeting

❦ Start and end on time.

❦ Have group members wear name tags during meetings until they know one another's names.

❦ Spend the first 5–15 minutes of the initial meeting introducing yourselves, if this is necessary. Otherwise, spend some time answering an icebreaker question (see samples below). In fact, you may use any good activity to help members get acquainted, interact with each other, or feel that they belong.

Icebreaker Questions

Icebreakers help your people become better acquainted over the course of the study. If the group members don't know each other well, choose questions that are general or nonthreatening. As time goes by, questions may become more specific or focused. Reassure the members that they may pass on any question they feel is too personal. Choose from these samples or create your own.

> *What do you like to do for fun?*
> *What is your favorite season? Dessert? Book?*
> *What would be your ideal vacation?*
> *What exciting thing happened to you this week?*
> *What was the most memorable activity you did with your family when you were a child?*

Name three things you are thankful for.

Imagine that your home is on fire. What three items would you try to take with you as you escaped?

If you were granted one wish, what would you wish?

Name the quality you appreciate most in a friend.

What is your pet peeve?

What is your greatest hope? Greatest fear?

What has been your greatest accomplishment? Greatest disappointment?

The Discussion

In discussion, members should interact not only with you, the group leader, but with one another. Usually you will start the ball rolling by asking a question to which there is more than one single acceptable answer. You are also responsible for keeping the discussion on track because if it gets out of hand and rambles, it loses much of its value.

Here are some guidelines for leading discussion:

❧ Maintain a relaxed, informal atmosphere.

❧ Encourage everyone to take part, but don't call on people by name unless you are sure they are willing to participate.

❧ Give members enough time to reflect and answer a question. If necessary, restate it.

❧ If someone is shy, ask that person to answer an opinion question or another nonthreatening question.

❧ Acknowledge any contribution, regardless of merit.

❧ Don't correct or embarrass a person who gives a wrong answer. Thank the person; then ask, "What do the rest of you think?"

❧ If someone monopolizes the discussion, say, "On the next question, let's hear from someone who hasn't spoken yet." Or sit next to the monopolizer to avoid encouraging her with eye contact.

❧ If someone goes off on a tangent, wait for the person to draw a breath, then say, "Thanks for those interesting comments. Now let's get back to . . . " and mention the subject under consideration; or ask or restate a question that will bring the discussion back on target.

❧ If someone asks a question, allow others in the group to give their answers before you offer yours.

❧ Summarize the discussion after the contributions cease and before you move on.

❧ Include in your meeting a time for sharing lessons which group members learn in their personal study time, praise items, prayer requests and answers, as well as a time for prayer itself.

PREPARED TO BE AMBASSADORS

OBJECTIVE

To help members see themselves as ambassadors for God in a foreign land.

PREPARATION

1. Prepare name tags for the group. On them write "Ambassador," allowing space after that word for members to fill in their names. Also write "Embassy address," below which members should fill in their own addresses.
2. Bring newsprint and markers or chalkboard and chalk.

GROUP PARTICIPATION

1. Distribute name tags as women enter. Discuss the definition of "ambassador" from Day 2, and brainstorm the responsibilities of such a person. What similarities do the women see to their own lives? Give those whose "embassies" are in the same part of town an opportunity to become better acquainted.
2. Encourage women to set personal goals—for example, of completing each lesson and showing growth in some particular way. They can write their goals in the front of their books.
3. Ask the women in the study to imagine they've just received this letter (1 Peter) in the mail. What would be their first impressions of what God had to say?
4. Help women locate places listed in 1 Peter 1:1 where first-century Christians were scattered. (Remember that some Bibles include maps of Bible lands.) Then ask members whose families are scattered to tell where they live and the results of being scattered. Besides home, where else do women in the group spend their time? (Day 2) Have volunteers read the notes they wrote to first-century women.
5. Read 1 Peter 1:1-12. Direct the women to discuss in small groups the outfits they would wear and the four ways God has outfitted them to live in this world (Day 3). How does God's outfitting prepare us for action and victory? Share results.

6. Come up with a group definition of "trial" (Day 4). How has the truth expressed in 1 Peter 1:8-9 helped members during times of trial?

7. Ask one volunteer to read Isaiah 7:14 and 53:3-6; then, portraying Isaiah, she should tell which prophecies he couldn't understand. Have a second volunteer read Matthew 1:18 and 1 Corinthians 15:3-4 and explain to "Isaiah" the prophecy's fulfillment (Day 5).

8. List words from 1 Peter 1:1-12 that point out how privileged we are and how the truths they describe influence our lives as resident aliens and ambassadors. Direct women to each choose one word and write it on their name tags. Suggest they save their tags as reminders.

CALLED TO BE HOLY AND OBEDIENT

OBJECTIVE
To explore God's call to be holy and obedient.

GROUP PARTICIPATION
1. Read 1 Peter 1:13-23. Have the women share what gets them off to a good or bad start in the morning (Day 1). Discuss the three ways Peter urges us to be prepared. Ask for reasons why following through is hard, but also for helps the women have found.
2. Discuss holiness by asking these questions based on Day 2:
   - ❦ Which of your parents do you resemble, and how?
   - ❦ Define *conform*. Give illustrations of what you mean.
   - ❦ Which definitions of holiness are most enlightening? How does conforming to God's Word produce holiness in us?
3. Ask a volunteer for an item from her purse; then charge her a dime to get it back. How does she feel? Have someone explain to the group how that depicts redemption — the fact that God owned us but bought us back with the death of His Son. What facts about redemption does the group see in Colossians 1:13-14?
4. Have volunteers read their responses as slaves who were made free, plus their notes of praise and thanks (Day 3). Ask women to cite key words in 1 Peter 1:18-19 and explain their significance. In groups of two, have women read those verses to one another.
5. The author wrote, "My responsibility was to keep choosing to live in the sparkling, new nature God had provided." Have the women share problems they meet doing this and how they handle them.
6. Share answers from Day 4 describing a relationship of brotherly or sisterly love, and a time the women received sacrificial love. Read Romans 5:5 and explain why we can show love even in trials. From their experiences and yours, discuss what sometimes must happen so that we can be loving in hard times.
7. Read 1 Peter 2:2. Ask women who've raised babies to describe the early eating habits and weight gain of their babies. Have them put Peter's message into their own words.

CHOSEN TO BE LIVING WITNESSES

OBJECTIVE
To better understand what it means to be a living witness for God.

PREPARATION
On newsprint or chalkboard, draw a wall of stones with a large cornerstone, as described in 1 Peter 2:4-8.

GROUP PARTICIPATION
1. Have volunteers tell when they entered a personal relationship with Christ. What gemstones do members think illustrate His qualities, and why? Ask the women what experiences they have had recently that make them glad Jesus is a living Stone.
2. Label your drawing's cornerstone. Then, as the women call out the names of biblical Christians who are part of the spiritual building, write the names on the other stones. Add names of contemporary women too. Ask why this is a "living building."
3. Have the women discuss in groups of four these matters of their priesthood from Day 2 and *Reflections Along the Way*.
    a. Why are women called priests?
    b. What are the responsibilities of women priests?
    c. What would help Christian women accept this concept?
    Come together as a whole group to report findings and discuss opportunities to act as priests in our world.
4. Allow a few minutes for members to find truths in Day 3 that motivate them to be compassionate toward those who see as foolish the need for a personal Savior.
5. How can women be living advertisements for God? (Day 4)
6. Have volunteers share their "good" fictional characters (Day 5), and justify their choices. Read Galatians 5:16-26. Discuss the origin of goodness and why it is hard to acquire. Ask members what women have modeled goodness to them. Have two persons act out 5:25 by walking around the room in step. Discuss implications.

CITIZENS AND WORKERS

OBJECTIVE

To learn practical ways to be better citizens and workers.

PREPARATION

1. Bring newsprint and markers or chalkboard and chalk.

2. Gather newspapers enough for everyone.

GROUP PARTICIPATION

1. Read 1 Peter 2:13-25. From Day 1, come up with an accurate definition of "submit," including words from verse 17. What two reasons are given for submitting to governmental authority? When should you refuse to do so? Invite a volunteer to role play a politician taking an unpopular stand on an issue, and a second volunteer to disagree with him while still showing respect.

2. Divide the women into small groups of three or four and distribute newspapers. Have the small groups scan them to generate ideas on how Christian citizens can fulfill their civic responsibilities (for example, be informed, vote, communicate with legislators, write letters to the editors of local papers about issues). Have the whole group discuss problems and solutions in acting as good citizens.

3. Have the women read and discuss the information they would include in a "Christian Employee's Manual" from Day 3. Based on their suggestions, have them formulate a personal code which you will write on the newsprint or chalkboard.

4. As workers in the home, how can the women apply the code above? What changes for the better might occur? What ways can we show honor and respect to those with whom we work, even when the other is clearly in the wrong? From Day 4, compile a list of ways Jesus was a role model. Share answers from the last question of Day 4.

5. Give time for women to prayerfully reflect on 1 Peter 2:24; then have them turn to someone nearby and talk over why the verse motivates them to be better citizens and workers. They should name the help to improving that the verse describes.

MAKING LIFE COUNT IN FAMILY RELATIONSHIPS

OBJECTIVE
To discover ways to live a God-honoring life at home.

PREPARATION
1. In a Bible dictionary or a book on life in Bible times, look up descriptions or illustrations of women's dress from that period.
2. Bring one uninflated balloon for each person.

GROUP PARTICIPATION
1. Give each woman a balloon to blow up and tie. After each shares her sentence completions from Day 1, she breaks her balloon.
2. Read 1 Peter 3:1-7. Divide women into small groups to review the definition of submission as it applies to wives; list obstacles women face in submitting; discuss (using information from Day 1) whether they should express their opinions or not; decide to whom they are to submit, and how; and discuss whether single women submit in different ways than married women. Share ideas.
3. From information in Day 2 and your own research, discuss fashion in Bible times. Ask how fashion and the concept of modesty have changed during our own lifetime. According to Scripture's guidelines, what fashion statement should a Christian woman make?
4. Listen to members' descriptions of a beautiful woman. Review the 10 boldface subheads in *Reflections Along the Way*. Which of them do the women think they need to pursue to become more beautiful? Have members give verbal clues one at a time about the Old Testament women they most admire while the others try to identify them (Day 3). Pinpoint why these women are so admirable.
5. What have the women learned about being Christian wives from Sarah's ups and downs? (Day 4) What do they think she could have told Abraham when he asked her to do questionable things?
6. Ask volunteers to play the parts of wife, husband, child, and other family members and tell their roles in making the family relationship work (Day 5). Then discuss *Day by Day with God*, Day 5.

WHEN IT'S HARD
TO BE FAITHFUL

OBJECTIVE
To find ways to become more faithful witnesses of Jesus Christ.

PREPARATION
1. Bring a slip of paper to give each member.
2. Bring newsprint and markers or chalkboard and chalk.

GROUP PARTICIPATION
1. As women enter, have them write their sentences suitable for calligraphy (Day 1) on the newsprint or chalkboard.
2. Read 1 Peter 3:8-22. Have the members share one way they would change how they handle difficult persons (Day 1). Review the four instructions. How could they improve the women's situations?
3. Read the sentences members wrote on entering. Take comments.
4. Have members create, in small groups, skits where a Christian witnesses to a non-Christian. One member describes the scene while two others act it out. Discuss each skit before going on.
5. Give each woman a slip of paper on which to complete: "One reason it's hard for me to witness is . . . " Members should not sign their papers. Collect them, read each, and ask for group input.
6. Ask for volunteers to form a panel to address issues regarding conscience (Day 3), such as how the conscience learns what is moral or immoral; when it endorses evil behavior; why a clear conscience is vital to remaining faithful; how to develop and maintain a more godly conscience. Ask for input from the others.
7. While one person pantomimes "Noah" building the ark, have "passersby" mock him. Tell members to answer for Noah, using each situation to witness. Then discuss how our world is like Noah's, and give conversation starters we can use to witness to specific people, such as baby-sitters and neighbors (Day 4).
8. Poll the women to find out which portion of Day 5 was most helpful to them. Read 1 Peter 3:15 and ask volunteers to describe the hope that is in them. How does it motivate them to be faithful witnesses?

CHRISTLIKENESS IN SUFFERING

OBJECTIVE
To consider the biblical teaching on suffering and formulate responses to it.

PREPARATION
1. Bring newsprint and markers or chalkboard and chalk.
2. Provide a straight pin and a three-inch circle cut from paper for each woman.

GROUP PARTICIPATION
1. Pass out straight pins and circles. State that, in order to keep the topic of suffering in mind, each woman should draw a picture of her face when she is suffering, then pin it on.
2. Read 1 Peter 4:1-9. Define the kind of suffering referred to in this passage (Day 1). Brainstorm the various ways women in our society might be persecuted for their faith. Use illustrations from Day 5 and ask for others.
3. Discuss *Day by Day with God*, Day 1. Say that we depend on prayer more than anything when times are tough. Ask volunteers to share a time when prayer got them through a trial. Go over specific things for which to pray (Day 2). Have the women talk in pairs about the subjects of prayer they need to focus on.
4. Ask the question from *Reflections Along the Way*, "Why does suffering come as such a slashing surprise?" Have women tended to believe a myth about the Christian life? Emphasize that we must be ready to suffer.
5. Hospitality can help alleviate others' suffering. Divide the women into small groups and instruct them to compile ideas for practicing hospitality with a minimum of time, work, and housecleaning. Exchange ideas when small groups come together; then urge members to each choose one idea, implement it soon, and report on it. How does offering hospitality help the offerer as well?
6. On newsprint or chalkboard, list the spiritual gifts of the women in your group. Read 1 Thessalonians 5:11 and discuss ways each

spiritual gift could be used to help hurting Christians.

7. Have the women pair up and answer these questions (Day 4):
   - ❦ Why do Christians suffer?
   - ❦ What does God want to accomplish?
   - ❦ How are we to respond and why?

Have the group sum up what we can know about Christlikeness during suffering from *Reflections Along the Way*. Instruct the women to turn their paper faces over and draw an expression they can wear during suffering because Christ is in them. Point out that, since we are human, pain may erase that expression at times; but because of His grace, it will return.

DISCIPLING AND BEING DISCIPLED

OBJECTIVE
To gain a fresh perspective on leadership and discipleship.

PREPARATION
Bring newsprint and markers or chalkboard and chalk, and paper for drawing.

GROUP PARTICIPATION
1. Ask for volunteers to share a time when the church helped them, and a time when it failed to help them (Day 1). Why is it important to be someone who helps others in the church?
2. Read 1 Peter 5:1-7. Talk about chances for women to be leaders in the church. Review qualities in 1 Timothy 3:2-7 as they apply to women (Day 1). Do a leadership profile based on this passage.
3. Write a definition of "one who disciples" on newsprint or chalkboard. Divide the women into small groups and have them list parallels between a shepherd and a discipler (Day 2 and *Reflections Along the Way*). Pool answers from the group and discuss insights.
4. Ask the group how women can discern which ministry they are to undertake when they are so busy. Ask members who've been overburdened to tell what they've learned.
5. Have volunteers read their answers to *Day by Day with God*, Day 2. What have they learned about discipleship from Jesus? (Day 3)
6. Small groups will analyze Titus 2:3-5, review Day 4, and discuss:
   ❦ Who would you categorize as "an older woman"?
   ❦ What are the qualifications to teach?
   ❦ What subjects might be most important today?
   Pool answers as a whole group and decide what members of this group could teach one another from their experiences.
7. Instruct the women to draw childlike pictures of how they felt when someone pointed out a flaw of theirs. Have them review Day 5 and caption the picture so as to remind themselves of the importance of learning humility. Artists will share their drawings.

STANDING FIRM

OBJECTIVE

To learn from one another more about defeating Satan, so that we can stand firm.

PREPARATION

1. Bring newsprint and markers or chalkboard and chalk.
2. Bring a ball of yarn for the final activity.

GROUP PARTICIPATION

1. Read 1 Peter 5:8-14. At what time of day and under what conditions are women most vulnerable to temptation, and why? What name of Satan best describes the way he acts in their individual lives? (Day 1) Explain answers.
2. Review comparisons between a lion and Satan in *Reflections Along the Way*. Discuss myths about him which women may have believed and the results. What problems have women had defeating him?
3. Direct the women to form small groups and go over the checklists they made based on Ephesians 6:10-18 (Day 2). Since armor is no longer in use, tell the groups to make sure they understand the specific spiritual preparation to which each piece of armor refers. Go over checklists as a whole group. Write key points on newsprint or chalkboard in brief phrases.
4. Ask how our attitudes toward suffering affect our vulnerability to Satan. Find out what the group has learned about standing firm from the person described in *Day by Day with God*, Day 3.
5. Plan a praise time using ideas and information from *Your Father Writes*, Day 4. Begin by having someone read *The Amplified Bible* version of 1 Peter 5:11; then ask volunteers to each read what they wrote for Day 4, question 3. Reflect together on ways in which praise keeps Satan from making inroads. Have members share their favorite ways to praise God when they're alone.
6. Allow the women a few minutes to talk in pairs about the goals they set in the beginning of this study and progress they have made. Ask what they can still accomplish.
7. How comfortable are the women demonstrating their love for one

another? Let them discuss ways they are most comfortable doing so, such as speaking a personal word to another or giving a hug. Allow them time for these expressions.

8. Form a circle and give the ball of yarn to someone. She should tell one insight she has gained from this study or a way she wants to apply a teaching. Then, holding on to the end of the yarn, she throws the ball to someone else. When that person finishes sharing, she holds the yarn at some point and tosses the ball. In this way, as the ball of yarn is thrown from one woman to another, it will form a web, indicating the women's interconnectedness to one another. Be sure to tell individuals they need not share if they don't wish to; they may simply throw the yarn to someone else. Close by singing a hymn.